Thyme on My Hands

Feb 2, 1999
To Brenna, who like a fine garden, brings joy and variety to my life. Wishing you many more wonderful years of gardening and friendship. Love,
Donna

Thyme on My Hands

by
Eric Grissell

Illustrated by
Taina Litwak

TIMBER PRESS
Portland, Oregon

Grateful acknowledgment is made to the publishers of *Garden Design* and *American Horticulturist* for permission to reprint (in somewhat different form) "Presently, in the Past" and "Kitchen Garden."

Copyright © 1986 by Timber Press, Inc.
All rights reserved.

Paperback edition printed 1994.

ISBN 0-88192-310-9

Designed by Sandra Mattielli
Printed in Hong Kong

Timber Press, Inc.
The Haseltine Building
133 S.W. Second Avenue, Suite 450
Portland, Oregon 97204, U.S.A.

Library of Congress Cataloging-in-Publication Data

Grissell, Eric.
    Thyme on my hands / by Eric Grissell ; illustrated by Taina Litwak.
       p.   cm.
    ISBN 0-88192-310-9 (pbk.)
      1. Gardening. 2. Gardening—Maryland.   I. Title.
    [SB455.G74 1994]
    635—dc20   94-37137
                                             CIP

Contents

To
Virginia and Coulter
for opening
the garden's gate

Preface

If you want to know "how" to garden you are advised to throw this book down straightaway and look elsewhere. The world has gone quite mad with such books, and there are far too many already on the market— some even written by people who know what they're talking about.

For quite a few years I have poked about in the soil myself. Enough years, at least, to know that I haven't the foggiest notion of what I'm doing. Let us be honest at the start, then, and say that herein you will find no answers to *"the* gardening questions of the ages." I have few answers to much of anything if the truth were known, and even when I think I might, someone has changed the questions. So let us not talk of answers, or even of questions. Let us talk, instead, of gardening, with a full understanding between the two of us that any information which might prove useful is merely an accident—I have not set out to be useful.

Physically, gardening requires a fairly strong and willing body. It requires even more an incredibly stubborn exercise of will. Its demands on the mind, however, are not overly excessive, and it is this factor which seems to suit me particularly well. In fact, so much of gardening's time is spent in pursuit of the repetitively inane that my mind often simply wanders off into its own dimension for want of anything better to do. Such distractions form the basis of the excursions which follow.

In terms of physical size or especial distinction, my garden must

1

be considered a modest suburban plot of little or no interest to anyone but myself. It sits about 20 miles (as the commuter drives) from the White House, but other than that scarcely differs from any other suburban plot. Its head gardener is a 7-to-4'er who battles dandelions (or ignores them mostly), once grew tomatoes for social acceptance, and wonders if life in an apartment might not have been more rational after all (it wasn't at the time).

As with many frustrated semi-urbanites who fight the battles to and from work each day, I often dream of retreat to the unperturbed wilderness. But one lives where one must (if one is not too adventurous, that is), and we need not flee the urban-suburban mass for imagined rural rewards. There is little to be gained, for example, by substituting pigs wallowing in the pansies for pooches grubbing up the petunias. Havoc is havoc someone once said, where it takes place is merely academic.

As the garden grows I have found that escape from daily troubles may be circumvented not by abandoning the suburban setting, but by retreating into it. This strategy works for three-quarters of the year, at least, but around here the garden closes down for the winter; I discovered early on that I did not care much for this situation. I would come home from work to find too much free time and no garden within which to spend it. And, as I soon discovered, too much time on my hands could be a very bad thing—very bad indeed. One may think, for example—a notoriously dangerous undertaking. Or one may mope about in idle depression. Or one may sit and write as I finally chose to do.

I write to dispel winter's blustery curse, to wander about the garden as freely in the pale of death as I do in summer's celebration of life. And if you should care to wander about the garden with me then please feel free to do so. Be forewarned, however, that we are apt to stray from time to time. As with many garden paths, mine are not bounded so much by primroses and pinks as by the mind.

1
Presently, in the Past

If a garden and a gardener's life be contemplated at all, as it eventually must, one seemingly enigmatic thought might quietly seed itself into some dusty, out-of-the-way corner of the mind. The thought concerns time and the enigma is this: the present is but a fleeting instant wherein one spends the least amount of time, but where one needs time the most.

The present, we are told, is the time to "stop and smell the flowers" or to "gather ye rosebuds." Yet presently, in my garden, I am doing well merely to find a plant finally in place, never mind stopping to admire its fragrance or pick its flower. Mine, you see, is a garden "under construction" and my first at that: there is scarcely time enough in present's meager moment to get on with anything at all. When I contemplate what has been done in the past few years and what awaits doing in the future, my mind fairly reels with progress. But when I think of the present . . . well, actually the less I think the better.

The present verges on one of the most difficult times to be in the garden. It is precisely when one is forced to notice the unprovoked invasion of creeping, long-legged grasses across well-trimmed, prim, proper, and totally unprotected borders; when one witnesses the belligerent dandelion prodigally slinging forth its outrageous arrows on all newly dug territories; when waves of normally well-behaved ivy suddenly rush forth to engulf the unsuspecting azalea; it is the time when one turns around to see Bruno carefully burying half a dozen primrose seedlings considerably deeper than the Primrose Society recommends (but in proper compliance with what cat society urges); and it is the time when every manner of wretched, crawling, slimy beast (I am not here referring to those children next door), plots to overtake the garden.

Present! Not necessarily a pleasant time in the garden, but rather a time to "see what must be seen." Gardeners sheltered by the goodness of past and future fear no evil, but those who wantonly live in the present cannot fail but to notice that splendid rhododendron, researched and searched for so longingly, so lovingly, now turned to matchsticks; that rose so lush with leaves, so well trained and pruned, thoroughly ripped to pieces by invading beetles; the rockery, so patiently weeded only minutes before (didn't I just spend hours sprawled inelegantly over the ground with ice-pick in hand?) now smothered in the purple passion of violets, everything in their path gasping for a breath of air and relief from the cleistogamous heat.

"To see what must be seen," that is the first law of the present. The instant requires such sacrifice, such valor on the part of the gardener. And it is difficult, to be certain. But not as difficult as the second law of the present that one must "do what must be done." And it seems as if something *always* must "be done" in the present. Those little bunches of violets, forever in the wrong place, must be bullied out of the ground so that favored dianthus and sprawling thyme may better catch the sun. To the weed a violent death to be certain, but a timely one, for all the heavy-handed bully has done is to insure the spread of never-ending seed all about the rockery, not to mention the little bits and pieces of root and stem which always remain to renew the untidy villain.

And for the once courtly rose what must be done? Why, everything, of course! Which is one clue to my lack of appreciation for the queen of thorns. I cannot guess why Japanese beetles are so fond of this vicious plant, but I do greatly respect their appetites. Overnight they can reduce the grandest dame to the raggedest pauper. And herein lies the true problem of the Japanese beetle; certainly not their destruction of roses for I should plant a whole pasture of roses in homage. No, the problem is that once the favored food is gone, what next? Again, everything. Now something *"really* must be done" or everything will go. And what of the rhododendron, that pile of spent, burnt sticks? In the present what can be done to keep the blight from turning such beautiful green leaves and fawny twigs into firewood? What can be done to keep the creeping borer from eternal, internal rasping as it slices the life from each twig?

Well, how should I know? I turn from the present at every chance, choosing to live in the past or future where these problems do not exist. But each rational gardener must at last face his own crises of the present, and unhappily unleash upon the wind the oft-uttered plea, "What do I do now?" And with that the gardener of the present has instantaneously wreaked havoc upon his complacency if not his garden, for lurking in the background—under every book, magazine, and garden column—is someone who knows exactly "what to do".

There are books, books, and more books to tell one exactly "what to do"; so many books espousing so many answers that one simply begins to grow numb lest one do the wrong thing. One drifts into the time-warp of indecision. Perhaps a little compost made from yak manure—steam sterilized with herbal tea—might perk up those petunias. Or lilting lullabies drifting softly through the herbaceous border might cure that pesky mildew. Might not a modicum of polite conversation (excluding, one hopes, world news and dismal weather reports) encourage a sorely wounded saxifraga back to health. How about raising the beds, or planting under pyramids, or soilless soil, or soilless water, or planting by the square foot, or under carpets (has anyone, I wonder, specified Oriental carpets for Chinese cabbage), or using drip irrigation, or wicks, or wands, or whatevers? Really! One would be led to believe that plants knew nothing of growing on their own without first reading about how it was to be properly done.

If books can't solve one's present problems, how about the garden columns of newspaper or magazine, or even radio and television? Here one reads (or hears) in seasonal unison, from every source, exactly how to plant daylilies, or irises, or rutabagas in excruciatingly morbid detail. Authors have used every word imaginable merely to say, "Dig a hole in good soil and plant the damn thing." Even my favorite television program, "The Victory Garden," has of late fallen in my esteem. I mean, just how many times does one need to learn how to plant carrot seeds? I don't even like carrots. (I still watch, however, when they plant potatoes. I like potatoes.) The serious gardener certainly does not need this constant badgering from the media.

Should one enjoy this sort of badgering (there are *those* sorts, I'm told) may I recommend the local garden center. These centers of unearthly delights specialize in those unfortunate gardeners stranded in the present; they guarantee that something will be gotten "done"— for a price, of course. Actually, one may be lulled into purchasing so many holey sacks containing virtually every conceivable sort of thing that nothing may ever be gotten at, let alone be gotten done! Bags of gypsum and sand to loosen the soil, lime to sweeten the soil, potting soil when soil-soil is not quite up to it. Here, too, are the bags of fertilizers with so many numbers one must keep a record book: fertilizers for promoting foliage, for coaxing flowers, for stimulating roots; fertilizers for acid-loving plants, for house plants, for tomatoes, for vegetables . . . something to stimulate every sort of perverted passion to which a plant might succumb.

Here, also are the arsenals of the present, to equip the gardener in his never-ending chemical warfare—insecticides, herbicides, rodenticides, fungicides, gas bombs, aerosols—where one mixes potent little cocktails for everything and everyone in the garden (including, I hasten to add having learned to read the label, one's self). And should one pursue the finer arts of gardening, one may see arrayed all of the glorious implements the present calls for if one can but bear to look— devices to hack, pinch, cut, lop, shear, trim, prune, scythe, mow, bind, gag—and not always the plants.

But if the present is a hard master, gardeners may always turn to their true friends, the past and future. For they know that what has been done and what awaits doing take precedence over the present's distractions. They know that yesterday's compost makes today's flower which makes tomorrow's compost—all very orderly, very organized, one might venture, and not the least bit as romantic as the present's single red rose.

The work of a gardener, by definition as well as choice, is in the soil and of the soil and for the soil. While it is acceptable to romanticize flowers, one scarcely cares to bare one's soul by expressing the same sentiment about dirt. Although getting "back to the land" is, of late, a very "in" notion, as is being "in tune" with Mother Earth, I think one would be in serious trouble, indeed, if one were seen in the company of too much dirt on the pretext that it was "romantic."

Still, I like dirt. I enjoy digging holes, digging out the lawn to make flower beds, and I especially enjoy bastard trenching (what a gardening phrase, that). But most of all I like the sight, the smell, the feel of newly turned earth. And while ordinary, garden-type earth takes me as close to heaven as I should care to be, there is only one additional step for those wishing to enter paradise—compost!

I find the aroma and texture of freshly screened compost as invigorating as any field of flowers. There is a pungency and look which vividly recalls the gardener's past; for that is what compost is . . . a keeper of memories. There is first that all pervasive, overpowering woodsy odor of damp, moss-strewn streambanks and fern-covered logs—reminders of those cool, deep canyons of one's youth. This blatantly romantic odor shifts imperceptibly, but pragmatically, to last summer's lawn, 400 square feet of inverted sod, and the backbreak of middle age. Most recently added, the tang of horse manure, now smelling of mushrooms, reminder of that day last January. It was 28°, my nose ran, my head ached, and the manure and straw was steeped in urine. So was I, but who cared. One must learn to sacrifice for the garden.

Of the sight of compost much from the past may be recalled if one but has the courage. Those watermelon rinds and corncobs not yet unrecognizable (leftovers from that high summer dinner gathering . . . and the burned roast); bits and pieces of last year's gardening failures, still sufficient reminders that one doesn't know nearly enough . . . root balls of defunct rock plants (overwatered, underdrained), mummified seedlings (underwatered, overdrained); even remembrances of last year's successes, reminders that one may occasionally be too lucky—those cart loads of wisteria, ivy, and honeysuckle trimmings now looking like so much piano wire. (Roses would be classified here except for two rules I have: 1) never, never put rose trimmings in the compost heap, and 2) never grow roses . . . well, almost never.) There is that old, wrinkled potato once thought useless, now plumped-up with eyes white looking for the sun, and here, a handful of straw from last year's strawberry bed mixed with straw from an anonymous horse's bed. A white piece of plastic catches my eye. It says "Saponaria" and something else not quite legible. I'd lost that plant last May. Another grows in its place now. Here, too, are a few chunks of concrete; I'd broken my back over them nearly 3 years ago (I swore I threw all of the pieces over the fence). And a pile of wind-fall apples—now mummies—which had clattered off the tin roof during the night merely to attract yellow-jackets in the fermentation of next afternoon's sun. Little did I know that these would be the last of their kind. The mother died, you see. After half a century of being picked on, she just went to pieces, taking the fence, a piece of the porch, and a minor poke at my car. Had I known that was to be her final summer I would not have been so hard on her children.

A gardener knows that the brewing of all these bits and memories of the past will speak well to the future. Nothing will be lost . . . not a single blade of grass, not a decade of weeds, not a century of leaves. Neither the remembrances of past triumphs nor the corpses of almost forgotten failures will be lost. They are being stored and resorted into the future.

Herein, I suspect, is what separates a true tiller of the soil from his neighbor who is, unknowingly, a slave only to the present. For most owners of so-called gardens, I fear, are confined to a few square feet of earth for which they have little feeling. The soil merely has come with the house and is largely an inconvenience to be grubbed and weeded. In some instances the entrusted earth will be taken care of, in some cases not, but it will never be cared for. Instant plants in full bloom, direct from some over-nurturing greenhouse or garden center, will be installed in unprepared soil, in the wrong place, and the owner will be satisfied—at least for the moment—with the usual temporary results. The present will be mollified, the past and future virtually eliminated.

Yet for gardeners the past is somehow consoling. Bad things were not quite so bad as we had imagined at the time, and good things seem much better. In the future things will be quite their best ever. We can make of the future what we will, take from the past what we can, and try to enjoy the present—momentarily.

9

2
A Matter of Time

The writing of this chapter is necessarily a function of the present, that is inescapable. Yet it is of the past that I write. Quests are, after all, a matter of time, and time is of the questence in the garden.

My gardening lust began as a child, as I loosely recall, with a few nasturtium seeds planted behind a knee-high white picket fence in the back yard of our San Francisco apartment. It was a small yard—a city yard, after all—in the shadow of the Twin Peaks which have slowly turned to human ant hills. The garden was divided in two by a tall picket fence, the rear half of which was a vegetable garden in the Italian manner. Honest, that is. This area belonged to the owner and was off limits to mere tenants. The fore-garden was for real plants, but perhaps after 30 years I will be forgiven if I cannot recall what they really were; I just recall the nasturtiums.

Even now, when I look at nasturtium seed (which is, fortunately, not too often), I cannot believe that anything will ever come of these sadly puckered ova. How such things are devised by nature I shall never guess, nor do I particularly care. They *are,* and that is good enough for me. The exact reasoning must await a time when reasoning is no longer necessary, and then the caring will be gone . . . so I do not fuss much with such problems as wrinkled seed.

(I have tried, in my present garden, to grow nasturtiums—to search for lost youth, the head-doctors might say—but about all I've found has been aphids. I plant the seeds, the cotyledons split, and out come aphids. Which makes me wonder if I'm doing something wrong?)

In the garden of my childhood, my interest remained firmly fixed on nasturtiums, but fortunately this fixation was short-lived. In the second garden of my youth—this time across the great bay to the north—something considerably different from nasturtiums entered my view. The feature that I remember best about that garden was the bank of rocks which stretched across the entire front of the property. Being on the order of 4 ft. high, man-made, and sloping backward onto the hill, this bank was clothed in the most wonderful of plants (or so it seemed to me after living in an apartment): baskets of gold cascaded between boulders, splashing against the pinks and whites of rockcress; floods of ice-box plant (as we called it, though it was not the annual sort) needing to be whacked back if anything else were to survive; sweet, sweet alyssum casting seed about in frantic abundance. These are among the most common sorts of plants, actually, but fortunately when one knows no better, weeds are every bit as good as gold. You can imagine, perhaps, what alpine adventures awaited the small lad who maneuvered across this great moraine with its cataracts of bloom. It was, I think, a good introduction to rock gardening.

There are many gardeners, I suppose, who do not think much of rocks, especially in the garden. They curse their stony soil and probably with good cause. Yet gardeners who worry about a few stones would do well to pause momentarily and reflect upon the case of Bertha Damon. For here was a woman who had 250 acres of "stones," "more stones," and the "cussedness known as glacial till." Yet she managed to garden, wrote a book about the adventure (*A Sense of Humus* Simon and Schuster, 1943), and pointed out that Californians took soil for granted while New Hampshirians took granite for granted.

To those who don't garden it must seem more than slightly odd that one gardener will spend hard-earned cash to have 20 tons of rock trucked into his garden while another will spend hard-earned cash on 20 tons of dynamite to blast the rock out of the garden. If only the two would get together—but then that would not be "gardening."

There was another childhood garden—in a slightly later time but nearly the same place—where I grew the sorts of things that must be grown: the tulip and daffodil, sweetpea and pansy, daylily, iris, and pink. And where I grew to dislike the "Great American Sport" of cutting the

lawn. But mowing was where the money was, and one must eventually cultivate some sense of independence, mustn't one?

It was during this time, also, that I began to work in a great garden which rolled down a hillside 'til it came to rest at the edge of the little valley in which we lived. A gardener's garden it was . . . well, actually, two gardeners' garden, but they always seemed as one to me. Of this garden and its caretakers I shall say no more until Chapter 19, but it had best be noted here that the joy of working in this garden, and of knowing its encyclopedic proprietors, has been the basis for much of my own spiritual well-being.

There came a day—as there eventually must in every young lifetime in the garden of eden—when spirit was wrenched from complacency and the residue was shipped off to the distant shores of Florida. The first adult job had arrived, and the first opportunity for a garden of my own arose. It did not bode well, as they say.

Gardening in Florida was not entirely what I had expected from life. First off, I had to live in an apartment. Not a good thing for a gardener. And while lush, subtropical conditions might seem enticing at first glance, what happens when reality strikes a poor fellow who has learned all of his gardening in a semi-mediterranean climate? In one word . . . rot! Every attempt at growing normal, childhood temperate plants resulted in half dead, wilted stems or corpses merrily rotting away in the warm humidity.

I tried to adapt, really I did, but what can one do on the balcony of an apartment? At one point I had nearly 60 pots full of one thing or the other—the truly handsome tropicals were stolen as fast as I grew them. I took pride in that, however, because it showed I must have been doing something right.

After several years it became obvious that I could not deny the baser instincts of my heritage; I became petulant and morose. Although I had purchased 5 acres upon which to start my first real garden, one could not, after all, live for long in a place where daffodils were unknown and crocuses merely croaked. Persons born of the temperate region cannot deny their rhythms any more than Floridians can shake the sand from their shoes. So I left for cooler climes.

Unfortunately, I found them in Washington, D.C. But before I am committed to an institute for the politically demented (say, for example, Congress or the White House), I should point out that this was not the spot on earth I would have chosen to live. No, it was purely a matter of opportunity and the fact that my job is so specialized that only in Washington could anyone figure out what to do with me. After seven years they still try, but it is actually a hopeless task.

With this move another opportunity arose to cultivate my very own garden. I had finally saved enough money to go into lifelong debt—that is, buy a house. I found, however, that I was faced with a decision of imponderable complexity. If I purchased a house I could afford there would be no land upon which to garden, but if I purchased land suitable for a garden I would not be able to afford a house. Inflation and recession were facts-of-life at the time, and facts-of-life tend to get in the way.

It must be true of nearly everyone who has ever entered the world of the living that one grows up with dreams and ideas of the way things will be. Rare, one would suppose, and possibly most unfortunate, are those few souls who truly see events unfurl as they had imagined. My own plans, for purposes of example, had been formulated "down the garden path" where book and mind had melded to form a barely comprehensible vignette of an incomprehensible world.

14

In my mildly blurred view of things, I saw rolling hills clothed in green, quaintly odd villages lost to time, gardens of immaculate conception, and homes swathed in stitches. In short, I pictured myself in an England of the 30s, or at least an approximation of what I thought it ought to look like.

Why this was so is probably a long, dark story which might give certain sorts of doctors something about which to speculate. They shall have to do so, for I know little enough about why thoughts are thought, and I usually care even less. I will touch ever-so-lightly upon the subject in Chapter 20 as a feeble sort of attempt at explanation. Otherwise you will just have to take my visions of reality on faith. Unfortunately, my own faith was sadly bruised when I took my visions to a realtor.

To a real estate agent there can scarcely be a more pathetic sight on earth than a client with delusions in one hand, downpayment in the other, and visions of an English cottage surrounded by Victorian grandmothers. And this in Washington, D.C.! I possibly destroyed the poor realtor quite beyond repair. She did, as a matter of record, resign from the realty profession shortly after I made a purchase—which says something about the way things were—but I'm not certain exactly what.

In three months of intensive house-hunting, garden-stalking, and excessive depression (it was winter, after all), I nearly destroyed 20 years of dreams, the goodwill of both the realtor and the relatives upon whom I was freeloading, and the faith of the empire. Not bad, actually, for only three months.

I still have not found the courage to relive this chasm in detail for it was not the least bit clear even at the time, and intervening years have done nothing to penetrate its shroud. A few things stand out, however. It was winter, that I do remember; January, February, and March to be precise. Dark and dreary and cold and ice-covered. I can recall computer printouts of "majestic flagstone terraces," "thrilling out-door living spaces," and "delightful gardens"; which liberally translated meant four tottering flagstones set among a back yard of bare dirt and yews—beside which ran a six-lane highway. Thrilling it might have been, perhaps even majestic to those who worship the car . . . but delightful it was not. None of it. Until. . . .

Until one day, just when I was about to give up and return to an apartment way of life, I found a house. It certainly was not what I had dreamed of for 20 years—this tiny Cape-Cod of brick painted blue—but then can anything ever be exactly what we imagine? Three months of snow, ice, rain, overwork, and over-inflation had all conspired to level English spires into American practicality.

The house, a simple 40-year-old box, sat on ⅓ of an acre of what charitably could have been called "lawn." A few large trees were thrown in for effect. Exact and gory details can await later chapters, but the "grounds" in March could readily be described as a brownish palette dotted with gray skeletons—a scene marvelously enhanced by the overcast and starkly shawdowless day adding just the right dash of spirit to the whole affair. I sought out the neighbor's mailbox to see if, by chance, it might read "The Adams' Family." Reassuringly it didn't.

For anyone not particularly intrigued with prospects thus far, I believe the only reasonable operative words are "one-third acre." This says it all . . . at least with my budget, in the Washington area, and 20 miles from work. Money isn't quite what it used to be, but people *are*— certainly more than they used to be; the combination is tough on gardeners who conspire to expansive thoughts in the vast wasteland of urban sprawl called suburbia.

In the end it was compromise which won out. A modest home on a fairly large lot is not to be scoffed at in these parts. The rear yard looked out across 6 acres of swampy field that were the backyards of several distant neighbors. I hoped (fervently) that the area would be too much trouble for anyone to want to build upon (true to date). My neighbors to one side had an acre and to the other, one-third. Across the street sat 2 acres of grass with a house on it (now three houses rest there). All in all an acceptable setting, but rather small for the arboretum I had envisioned.

Yet, again, compromise was the key note as I threaded my way between still slippery spots of ice and increasingly slippery spots of mud. Here *was*—I cajoled myself—a nearly blank canvas upon which to begin a floral painting. A bit small, true. But blank. I would simply have to downscale my plans. It would be a great challenge. After all, anyone with unlimited ground could create an arboretum or botanical garden. Anyone, that is, who was perennially and perpetually endowed and had nothing but time on their hands. And that obviously left me out.

3
Greengrocers

And now it is time to begin the garden! It really is. Except for one minor detail which is not very complicated but somehow must be addressed before I can really "get on with things." It strikes at the very heart of gardening and I must lay it to rest for both of our sakes.

I am not certain when it occurred, but sometime during my trek from childhood nasturtiums to new-found sanctuary, the word "garden" had become synonymous with "vegetable." I might have been off weeding the irises when it happened and would not have known it to this day except for an event in July of 1982. Until then I had always imagined myself to be a gardener, but upon that fateful day I ventured into the garden and found it completely gone. At least by any other name it was missing and I was no longer its caretaker.

The reason for this abrupt turnaround was found in a *Newsweek* cover story called "The Joy of Gardening" in which the word "flower" was not mentioned, or even alluded to. Apparently the national joy of gardening consisted entirely of vegetable beds. I was so annoyed by this assertion that I immediately wrote to the editor and accused him of nationally deflowering the American gardener . . . and in public view. Apparently he agreed because the letter was published without rebuttal.

As if to emphasize my confusion, the next year I joined Gardens for All (*The* National Association for *Gardening*, emphasis mine) only to discover that its prime objective was to help "people be successful food gardeners." I then became convinced that the greengrocers were plotting to take over our gardens.

I suppose the change had been creeping up on me slowly and without my knowledge, but in retrospect I now know that I was continually falling victim to the "greengrocer syndrome." There had been clues, perhaps, which portended disaster, but I had blissfully ignored them. For example, when I would ask one of my gardening friends how their *garden* was growing, they would always answer "the tomatoes are doing well this year." The tomatoes always came first and often were the *only* plant mentioned at all.

Whether this syndrome is a factor of the age in which we live (nouveau victory garden, avant gardening, and all of that) or whether it is personal paranoia, I know not. But I don't like it. Not one bit. When I ask someone about *their* garden I am asking about *the* garden not the "vegetable" patch. Invariably, however, the person launches off in irrepressible, enthusiastic detail about his swiss chard, his potatoes, his spinach, or his rutabagas (well, rarely about his rutabagas . . . that might even be entertaining).

Not that I have anything against vegetables, mind you—it's just that I can't grow them all that well. I know this is some sort of sin, and perhaps even un-American, but I simply cannot get them to grow. My fingers are not green, so to speak, in this direction. I have been known to give it a try, but it was under much external pressure and certainly with profound internal protest, and I do not care much to admit it. Nor do I often brag about the fact. But I did once grow vegetables for social acceptance, and I shall tell you how I did it. My story is not a pleasant one, but it can be no more horrifying than the current tales of growing vegetables under carpets, or in pyramids, or in the intensively French manner, all of which have received rather more attention than is either necessary or even healthy.

To begin this story I must go back to the very first summer of my newly acquired garden (or whatever it is called these days). When my friends came to visit for the first time the one question they always asked was, "what are you going to grow in the garden?" Without hesitation I would launch into my theories of gardening, my ideas of rock gardens, herbaceous borders, historical gardens, and the like, only to be received in absolute, bored silence. "But what about the tomatoes?" they would ask. I sensed immediate social disgrace if I did not answer correctly.

"Oh yes," I managed to mumble . . . mouth as dry as my pocket, sweating out a response which would certify me as worthy of their friendship. "The vegetables, did I forget to mention them? Careless me. I mean everyone has vegetables now, don't they? I just assumed you knew. It goes without saying now, doesn't it, that somewhere I would have my vegetable patch." (They look slightly more kindly upon me.) "Oh yes! It goes without saying. It is simply understood. No question. You know." (They positively beam at me. Everywhere, smiles.)

So now I was lost. Truly lost. Before society's stern command and being rather weak of will, I recovered my garden plans from under the sofa to reconstruct them in such a way as to find a little bit of land suitable for sacrifice on the altar of the greengrocer. I searched for hours, days, endless weeks, and all merely to find a bit of spare ground. Finally I hit upon a tiny square of ground, covered with ground-ivy and grass at the base of a 30-year-old silver maple. Just the place, I thought, nothing will grow there but good enough to fulfill my obligation to social demands.

Never having grown vegetables before, except for radishes (whose only value is that they grow fast and so make good compost), I did what I usually do when I don't know what I'm doing—I began to

read. Perhaps this was my basic mistake, you see, because I came upon a fascinating book which did "it" the Chinese way. I greatly admire Chinese cooking, and this method would produce, if the illustrations were to be believed, the most aesthetically extraordinary sight on earth. Here was my chance to combine the dreaded chore of growing socially acceptable tomatoes and produce ingredients necessary to practice my cooking, while creating an ocular vision of major proportion. It could not have been better planned if I had thought it all out by myself.

Out came the plans, pencils, erasers, measuring tapes, string, stakes, spades, forks, and rakes. My plan was simple. There were to be three narrow beds, each 4 × 12 ft. separated by narrow paths. Each bed was to be double-dug and mounded, and never to be walked upon again. All work was to be done from the little paths so as not to compact the soil. This was exactly what the Chinese-way said to do, so I was going to do it.

The next step was to dig. Fortunately, I did at least one thing correctly: I started as far away from the tree as possible. The soil was of an extremely rich coffee color with the texture of sandy loam. I was profoundly impressed with its potential (much too good for vegetables, I thought, but kept from my friends). This area was, as I later discovered, the point to which the entire neighborhood drained, and because of this it was quite sedimentary in nature. Probably the best soil from all of my neighbors' yards had collected here.

At the time I commenced digging, the soil was quite dry and fairly workable except, of course, for the nails. Had I mentioned the nails before? Well, actually the nails were not really quite as bad as all that . . . they all looked about the same, they varied little in size, and all had the same rusty orange color. They were probably really quite good for the soil. Once used to them, it wasn't all that difficult to separate the nails from the worms with rigor mortis. No, I think the nails were not actually the problem. At least nowhere on a par with the glass.

I'm not certain, exactly, what sort of garden had been here in times gone by, but it seemed as if previous owners had it in mind to grow the vases first and then the flowers. Someone had gone to a great deal of trouble to spread out evenly all those bits and pieces of dishes, bottles, and sundry ceramics. There was an endless variety of shapes and sizes, none of which vaguely looked the same. Some were even invisible. I found the latter by the little red stains they left on my fingers as I grubbed through the soil.

After the excessive abundance of glass, came the customary rocks, pebbles, cobblestones, chunks of concrete, and objects d'art. These latter finds were the least common but the most interesting part of the digging. The little tin soldier (sadly modern and made of plastic), the toothpaste tube, toothbrush, coiled bits of wire, spark plugs, tobacco tin, plastic car, the odd button, marbles, a rusty pocket knife, and the obligatory penny or two. I kept a sharp lookout for buried jewels and gold, of course, but alas none were to be be found. Such is my life.

Evening after evening I dug from the time I arrived home until sundown. The rocks and chunks of concrete mounded up . . . first in buckets, then in cart loads. The nails, glass, and other spoils were carted to the trash. Two days, four days, a week, a weekend, two weekends, and finally I was two spits deep by 4 ft. wide by 12 ft. long. My first bed was done. A long, beautifully raised mound of rich, chocolate soil. The struggle certainly would have been worthwhile had I been planting a bed of irises or of daffodils, but Chinese cabbage? I began to wonder. Social pressure, however, is an awesome thing, and convinced of impending inferiority and reduction in rank, I pressed onward with my "revised" plans for the second and third beds. These were to be dug only one spit deep.

On the second bed I breezed along easily for awhile. The glass thinned out as did the what-nots (nails, however, continued to plague me, as they do to this day . . . I think they must be hermaphroditic). About half-way through this bed I hit the next major obstacle, or rather its roots. I was losing patience at this point, and no inanimate piece of ground was going to have the better of me after two weeks of ruined evenings' and weekends. So I set off to the nearest hardware store to procure the longest axe I could carry. I wasn't quitting until all three beds were dug. The second bed was axed-out in near record time and lay parallel to the first in but a few evenings' worth of work.

The third bed was undertaken with a recently reviewed, newly revised second plan of attack. This bed would be dug as deeply as the shovel would go . . . to hell with it. I have only so much time to devote to tomatoes, and I had already exceeded it by eons. The spade was poised for the first cut, my right foot gave a mighty push. The shovel sliced 1/16 in. into the ground, recoiled off a tree root, and shortened my left boot by an inch. That was all I could take. I stalked to the shed, gathered an axe, saw, crowbar, and dynamite. In less than one day I had dug the last bed—and just as I'd planned: 4 ft. wide, 12 ft. long, and ½ in. deep. The surface bore the same appearance as the others which was good enough for the greengrocers if you asked me.

I now had three beds with nearly 150 sq. ft. of planting area (all right be particular if you must, so it was only 100 if you don't count the last bed). The temptation is great to outline the "planting scheme" for this masterwork of Victory Gardening . . . to expound at length upon such triumphs as Chinese cabbage, oriental onions, and the like, but I shall not so so. I forego this recital firstly because there are already far too many works which have done so, and secondly because of the floods.

The beds were designed, you see, to be raised and stay that way. My folly was the use of a Western garden book to build an Eastern vegetable garden. In the West, which has no rains in the growing season (or so I recall from childhood), a raised bed may stay raised. In the East, however, it never stops raining during the growing season (especially on weekends) and raised beds don't stay raised. At least mine didn't. They merely melted away as sheets of water poured down the street and across the neighbors' yards into mine.

As of this writing though, I am happy to report that all has ended for the best. I have confined the raised beds within lumber stays, I have dug drainage channels to divert the flood waters, and to sop up the excess water I have planted Louisiana irises and a bald cypress.

But most importantly, to divert the greengrocer's query "how does your garden grow?" I simply reply: "The rice harvest will be substantial this year. How about yours?" For some reason they seldom ask again.

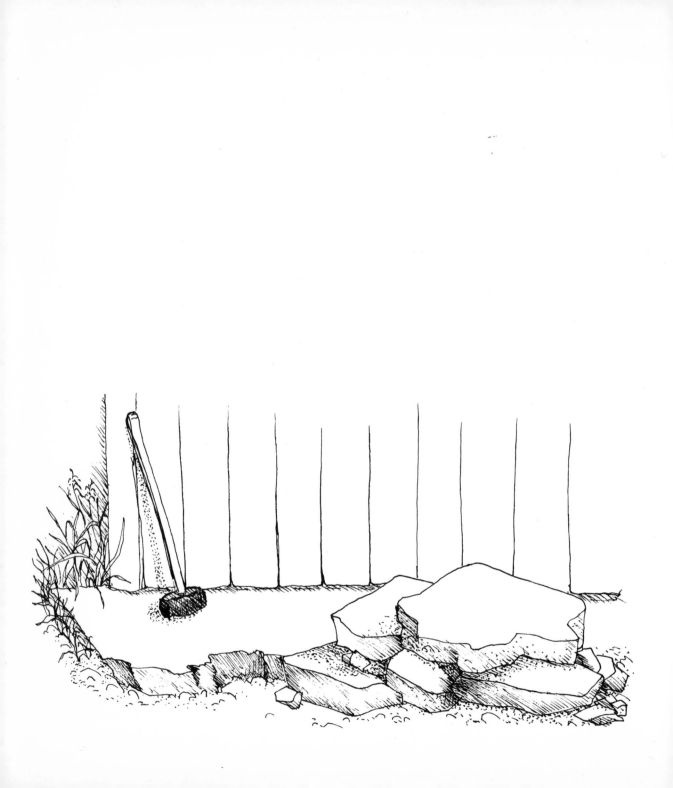

4
Of Indecision

The sound is of steel on concrete as I slowly beat a poor, misplaced slab of gray into tiny fragments. Weak muscles, made even weaker by unaccustomed labor, begin to wobble with fatigue and I carefully lay the sledge down. Free, at last, for a few moments from ringing ears and the projectiles which have managed to hit every bit of body except the protective goggles I wear; free from the concentration of aiming at as small a target as possible to make the strokes easier; and now, unfortunately free to ask myself why, in the midst of a broiling hot day, I should be doing such a silly thing at all?

I note mentally that some people are forced to do such labor for pay, or even worse, for penance, and I am doing it for recreation. In my case, the answer was relatively simple. I was doing one of the routine, day-to-day chores required of a newly acquired garden . . . namely rearranging the furnishings. In this instance I was evicting an unwanted slab of concrete merely because it was in the wrong place. The slab knew it, and I knew it, and so it had to go. Pity is, that if the person who originally put it there had known it, we both could have been saved some trouble. Which is just to say that if you want something done correctly you can always count on someone else not to.

So here I came, then, each evening upon returning from work, chipping away at an object for which I held no personal malice. Mauling it, as it were, until it should conform to my concept of its place in the garden.

When I first surveyed my new back yard there was little else except this slab. There was a large square of earth bounded by a fence-row and a few trees, there was a shed, and the remainder was lawn. Lawn is actually far too kind a word, however it does convey a general concept, if not the precise truth. There was, shall we say, a definite lack of something in the back yard ... well, nearly everything if I might be direct. There were no flowers or flower beds, no rock gardens, no vegetable garden, no paths, no pond, few shrubs, not even water taps. The obvious were obviously not there.

In the beginning—that is to say shortly before I created the nightly entertainment of smashing concrete into rubble—I used to come home and wander about the yard with measuring tape, paper, and pencil. This I fondly referred to as "planning." However, after many weeks of planning, I had scarcely more to show than some grid paper with a few essential components of my yard (i.e., size, shape, trees, shed, and slab). I was not progressing in what we might charitably call a positive direction until one evening toward the end of my first summer.

I had finished the obligatory course of pacing about the yard and standing near the concrete slab in the optional contemplating mode. As I stood contemplating what wasn't there, shifting from one foot to the other, it occurred to me that what I wanted most was simply some place to sit down. One of those fairly simple thoughts, I suppose, but the kind that inevitably gets one into trouble. As it happened, the only places to sit down were the lawn which ran up to the back of the house and the small concrete paddock that stuck out 8 ft. from the corner of the house. I chose the grass as the more comfortable alternative and settled down once again to contemplate the vastness of my holdings. But the more my mind envisioned the garden that was to be, the more my thoughts, prodded as usual from behind, struggled toward a place of more comfort and visibility. I needed a higher vantage point, not to mention the fact that my trousers were soaking up more moisture than I cared for.

And so it came to pass that I dragged an unwilling chair from the house to the yard, and having gained a box seat, it finally came to me in the end, so to speak, that I knew what was missing from my yard. It wasn't a garden, for the elements were all there in my mind awaiting liberation. What was missing, however, was a decidedly overdue introduction: I had a house, in its 40th year, and a barren yard in its 40th year, and neither had been formally introduced.

I'm generally not one for introductions, but the results in this

case were to far outweigh any misgivings I might have had. For the simple act was to unleash a torrent of ideas which were to culminate in "The Plan."

But first things first. With the formal introduction were created the first tentative links between the indoors of the house and the outdoors of the yard. Given time I could create a garden, but what good is a garden if it is isolated from the house? And of what use is a house if it be separated from the garden. One may as well live in an apartment. I wanted the house and the garden to be extensions of each other, not just neighbors. There was little doubt that something was needed to tie the two elements together. Something which would entice a visitor to step forth from the house into the garden as if it were just another room. Something to make the transition from home to garden more appealing (and safer) than a sudden drop-off from back step to lawn.

From the start there seemed only one plausible approach to take, but one which proved to entail endless chains of decision-making. The approach was nothing more than a simple terrace which would extend the firm, secure footing of the house into the otherwise open insecurity of the garden to be. The decisions, I naively thought, were threefold, and involved simply a choice of material, shape, and size. Nothing could be easier.

However, being a master of indecision and a graduate of the "study-it-first" school, I entertained myself for months with the possible alternatives to my choices. Should I, for instance, take the easy way out and merely extend the previous owner's attempt at solving the same problem by enlarging the concrete pad to encompass the whole back of the house? This would rather easily solve two problems at once, one of which was to create a terrace and the other to hide the small pad. Several weeks later, after much thought, I decided that the idea was quite a poor solution at best. I would only have turned a small square of concrete into a very large one, and then how would I hide that? I don't really care for concrete all that much, and the thought of more was not exactly to my taste.

My thoughts next turned to the elegant wooden decks of my youth—the ones which cover the hillsides north of San Francisco. It is often easier to rely upon how things "used to be" rather than to come up with new and innovative thoughts. So I decided upon the familiar. A nice redwood deck, impervious to water (which we have in abundance) and never needing maintenance, would be just the thing. The terrace would *have* to be redwood because maintenance of wood products (such as houses) is not highly rated on my list of priorities.

So a search began (as usual) for exactly the right materials, and I soon found out a thing or two. The first was that redwood grew on trees and they hadn't cut many on the East Coast that year. The second was that to get redwood to the East Coast apparently required shipment by first class mail. The cost was dear, if we might understate the case.

There were other woods, I soon came to learn, that were suitable for outdoor construction, but somehow pine treated with "heavy-duty CCA preservative to 0.40 lbs. per cu. ft. retention" was not my idea of what a terrace should be. In the end, as with many good ideas, wood was quietly eased to the bottom of the pile of choices, so to speak, and I began my search anew.

Next came brick. Thoughts were really evolving now. Here, in the fourth month of deliberation was a very clever choice. My house was made of brick and wouldn't it be natural just to extend the brick into the garden? My problem was solved! I started to investigate brick paths and brick walls and brick terraces and brick bricks. I talked to brick people. I bought bricks. I even practiced making a brick terrace 2 ft. square where the garbage can could sit. It was very nice, very nice indeed. And I mangled only one finger in the entire process.

But then, as is frequently the case, vague doubts began to set in. It happened one evening when I was invited to dine at a home which had a charming, quaint patio made entirely of brick, or at least parts of it looked like brick. Most of it, however, looked like moldy bread. Black, green, and white patches of sundry slimy algae and molds created interesting decoration to be certain, but given a little practice one could probably achieve the same results with rotten wood and at a third of the cost. While the colors were less than breathtaking, one could easily have had the breath taken from one as walking on the brick was akin to negotiating an icy sidewalk in leather-soled shoes. Not for the timid, one might say.

And then there was the general unevenness. Had the patio been made level at any time in its colorful life, I queried. "Certainly," was the reply, "flat as a deck." What accounted for the present unevenness I shyly asked? "Heaving," was the reply. No, I countered, I didn't mean the black and green stuff. "Heaving," they said, "you know, frost action." No, I said, I didn't know frost action. Where I came from frost was little white stuff that made pretty pictures on things. But I soon came to learn of the powers of positive heaving and what it can do to bricks and walks and things. And because heaving seemed to be an awfully regular thing hereabouts (what with Congress and all) I decided to redirect my search.

Six months after the initial inspiration to build a terrace, I was still scarcely anywhere near making even one of my three decisions as to size, shape, and materials, let alone all three of them. So I decided to take another approach to the problem . . . forget it. I find it often helps in a pinch. Instead I went off on a wild rock chase, which naturally was just the thing to solve my terrace problem.

Because one of my gardening plans was to build a rockery, I began to investigate a source of rocks. As with the terrace, my "study-it-first" approach was again invoked, and the indecision this time centered around what kind of rocks to use. As you will undoubtedly realize, having closely followed (one hopes) the sequence of events surrounding the phantom terrace, the story of the rocks is somewhat analogous and need not be told here. The point is this: a) there are no rocks around my home, b) therefore one must purchase same, c) therefore one must find a local rock store, d) I found five such stores, e) they had many kinds of rocks at many prices, f) I made many, many trips back and forth to decide which rocks to use, and naturally g) I discovered the material

31

with which to construct my terrace.

The law governing this type of phenomenon is what I call the "short-life" law, that is, the solution to one problem occurs only when another, even more difficult problem arises. Anyone wishing to calculate the permutations of this law will soon see that it is better not to live too long if one is susceptible to it.

What I found at the various rock stores (in addition to rock, of course) was a large selection of various sizes and shapes of thick, heavy flagstone. I like flagstone. It is very rock-like, whether in irregular or cut pieces. It goes well with real rocks and equally well with the outdoors or the indoors. It does not seem to harbor algae. It looks good with plants. In large pieces it is heavy and not so easily heaved as bricks. It is therefore easier for me to work with, being so awkward to handle that I must work slowly so as not to mangle any fingers.

And so it came to pass that the decision was made to use flagstone. There remained only some basic minor problems as to what to do now that I had chosen the material. Fortunately for me, and possibly the reader as well, I had been contemplating the size and shape of the terrace for nearly as long as I had been trying to find the material. (I have found it necessary to double or triple-up on thoughts like these due largely to the short-life law to which I fall easy victim.) As regards size, I had determined that the terrace would run the entire width of the rear of the house (30 ft.) and the depth would be about 25 ft. This seemed to fit well on the graph paper I used to map out my many plans. However, knowing the usual success of my plans, I got out the stakes as a precaution and marked off the entire plan on the ground. The paper plan obviously needed help! Much too big and monotonous, I thought. And rationally so, I found out, after calculating the cost of such an expanse of flagstone.

Out came the stakes again, and I pushed them in and pulled them out of the ground for several weeks before reaching a compromise between size and cost. But in so doing I discovered a shape that was at once more practical for my future plans as well as immeasurably more pleasing than a mere rectangle. The terrace would start at 12 ft. wide and run slightly more than halfway across the back of the house at which point it would flair out into an irregular hemioval of 23 ft. at the most distant point from the back door. At that point two or three steps would lead from terrace to garden. Because the yard sloped away from the house, the terrace would have to be built up at that point to make it level with the house, and a wall would have to be built around most of the circumference of the bulge.

The shape proved to be practical for two reasons. Firstly, because it provided a single, large lounging area (someday, I thought, I would even like to sit down and admire the garden) which would ultimately help divide the garden into two diagonal vistas instead of a single straight one. Secondly, because the narrow section was to be in front of a set of French doors which looked out over the garden. The doors were not yet present, but sitting inside the basement looking at the wall, I knew I wanted a view of the garden—but not a view of an immense stony flatness. The whole idea was to glimpse the verdant garden beckoning through glass doors, to approach the view (cautiously, if need be), to be lured out onto the narrow part of the terrace (which was merely part of the house and nothing to be afraid of), and then to move immediately towards the lounging area where comfortable chairs would entice the viewer onward and outward. The last thing I cared to create was a log-jam where doors met terrace as I am not overly fond of staring at hindquarters (at least in the garden).

Having finally divined the material and defined the size and shape of things to be, I was left with only one minor problem, possibly not even worth mentioning. I mention it, however, to infuse courage into those non-do-it-yourselfers, like me, whose fear of undertaking virtually any project prevents them from experiencing some of the finer disasters in life. The problem was elegantly simple, I wanted a terrace at least partially hemispherical (actually hemiovical, if such is possible) in outline, but I wanted to use rectangular and square flags to build it. I believe they use a similar problem in psychological testing—possibly with the same results as I created.

Working diligently with graph paper and cutout replicas of available flagstone shapes I arrived at a method of turning straight lines into curves while at the same time keeping all stones parallel. This was not a bit easy, not in the least, but it was such a useful optical illusion, and surprisingly provided me with an additional space of garden, that I shall pass up the patent rights and outline the terrace as it stood at this point (at least on paper):

The lounging area of the terrace was to consist of a more or less peripheral, step-like arrangement of flag, approximating a curve. The wall holding up the terrace would be a real curve, and the space between the wall and terrace would be filled with soil. By planting ground-hugging plants, low mounding shrubs, and perennials in the soil area I could round-off the flagstone "points" in a few years and no one could tell where flags stopped and wall started. It would be even more convincing if the wall were made of nearly the same material as the flags and so I decided to use stone. In this case Pennsylvania field stone which I happened to find on one of my many forays to the local and not-so-local quarries.

As envisioned, the stone would serve two purposes: one to hold up the terrace, which was a theory I thoroughly believed in and one of very few which proved to be true, and two, the unmortared stone wall would serve as a vertical garden for choice rock plants which would smother the wall in bloom (this theory, however, reads truer if the word "smother" is changed to "occasionally covered").

So now, 9 months after initial conception, a full-fledged plan was born, awaiting only the execution of the simple task of ordering materials. This accomplished, the trucks rumbled in, one by one, this one dumping 6 tons of rock and 500 sq. ft. of flagstone, another dumping 9 tons of gravel, and yet another 5 tons of sand—all on the driveway.

Then followed the not so simple task of getting all this stuff off the driveway and into the back yard. Which reminds me anew, painfully anew, that I was actually in the process of breaking ground—or rather concrete—when I started this chapter, and that something else was beginning to break at this point—namely my back.

5
. . . and Backbones

A garden must start somewhere, obviously, and the most logical place would seem to be the brainbone. But the human mind can do only so much and it is not always entirely helpful. It still comes as quite a shock to me that the brain willfully creates so much havoc for the rest of the body. Merely by producing a thought, perhaps lasting but a second in time, it can assure the body of days, weeks, or even years of wondrous sufferings.

For example, the mere conception of adding a flagstone terrace to my house, though created in milliseconds in some rusted, electrically shorted synapse of my mind, has produced countless hours of labor for another part of my body, namely my backbone (or what remains of it). Somehow, I believe evolution (or divinity, if you prefer) has sorrowfully failed us in this interaction: the brain should know the limits of our physical abilities. It simply does not know, or does not care, and I rather suspect the latter to be the case.

When one is younger, thoughts may occasionally arise (though this is by no means assured) which one may contrive one's elders to implement. This phenomenon relies for support on smallness of size, lack of muscle, sorrowful eyes, and a certain bravura which adults possess (but don't understand) and which children know how to manipulate. I have found that this power over others has waned by about 18 years of age (the eyes start to go, I think) and we are faced with three basic approaches to implement our own ideas. The first is certainly money, for it can (and does) purchase nearly anything: anything, that is, except good service. For this, one relies on the second and third options: namely one's friends and one's back. Both of these options, however, are on the fragile side and one must exercise tact when seeking the cooperation of either.

The gardener's friends are a precious resource and should not be taken too lightly. That is why I will eventually devote an entire chapter to them. But I borrow them from time to time to prove a distinct need for self-reliance on the part of the gardener. The point is that where friends are concerned one must always be aware of the "reciprocal work equation" which states that:

> If friend A does X amount of work for friend B, then friend B must do X amount of work for A, generally at the most inconvenient time possible.

Why this is so I do not know, but it is, and I accept it. It is one of the reasons I rarely ask anyone to help me. There is a corollary to this equation of course, which may be referred to as the "inverse back law" which states that:

> Two backs working in unison usually accomplish half as much as one back working alone.

I'm certain this has been proved rigorously and quantitatively in some scientific journal or other . . . the exact one escapes me. The effect is directly due to food diversions, baseball breaks, arguments over work habits, intellectual discussions (usually centered on some aspect of tomato culture), union rules, and gin. The exact order may vary, but the result is always the same: I could have accomplished more on my own. I generally consider the consequences of asking a friend for help and then do the work myself.

Money and friends notwithstanding, if I have a job to do I am generally left to the mercy of my own back. "Mercy," I suppose, is as good a word as any to describe what I'm left with most of the time; at least it is kind. This was my situation, then, after the trucks rattled away leaving behind a driveway totally obscured by rocks, sand, gravel and flagstone. But wishing to realize the creation of my terrace I was left with the clash of several ounces of backbone against roughly 30 tons of immovable objects.

Not much hope there, it would seem, but in the end everything was moved and almost arranged in its designated place. And the strength that guided it was absolute, pure enjoyment, fueled, to be certain, with uncounted infusions of gin and tonic.

If this sounds altogether too absurdly easy to actually have been accomplished, it is because I have left out the minor parts which might tend to discourage the normal do-it-yourselfer. I neglected to mention, for example, the year between the time I began and the time I finished—the FIRST time. Then there was the year between the time I started the second time and finished the second time. And did I mention the two years between the time I started the third time and finished—the THIRD time? I thought not. I figure if a job is worth doing once it may as well be done twice. Just for the practice.

The first two "restructurings" were undertaken to compensate for my inability to grade properly. I mean it was perfectly proper when I did it in the summer, but winter's ice has a way of expanding things and I was right back to heaving again.

The initial problem arose when the flagstones heaved up and blocked the storage doors on the porch. Ordinarily this would not have been a problem; I mean who needs a spading fork when the temperature is 16°? The real problem, actually, was the oil tank which was secreted behind the doors. It *was* a necessity at 16°. My first solution was to saw the bottom off one door, which worked, but not very well. Next I pried up the necessary flags on a relatively warm day. That worked, too, but eventually I had to remove a considerable number of stones and regrade the entire area in front of the doors.

Next came the problem of heaving, flooding, and ice damming in front of the French doors. When last I spoke of these doors they were of the imaginary sort. But during the interval between the first building of the terrace and the first rebuilding of the terrace, I succeeded in having a hole made in the basement wall, and a set of doors now looked out over the next cycle of impending doom.

The area directly in front of these doors turned out to be formed of the most amazing sort of silly-putty mud I've ever seen. When wet, the flags would quiver as if set on strawberry jello; when frozen, they heaved like the morning after; and when a thaw occurred, the basement flooded as if I'd planned it that way. And I hadn't, if you must know.

The following spring I removed all the offending flags, dug down another 8 in., removed all the roly-poly mud, added some drainage, backfilled with gravel and sand, and replaced the flagstone.

Amazingly, this halted the rolling, the heaving, and the flooding at least in the winter. The basement still floods in the summer, but only on those very rare occasions when it rains.

Lastly the problem of the new sewer line developed. I am really not up to that story just yet, as the repairs were only semi-finished about 2 weeks ago. Some stories become humorous, or at least moderately tolerable, only after certain intervals of time. In the case of the sewer I have not yet approached the proper time ... perhaps in the next book.

Let me just say that 200 sq. ft. of flagstone had to be removed (by me), then 100 cu. ft. of muddy backfill had to be removed (by me), nearly 100 cu. ft. of sand and gravel had to be put back (by me), and then 200 sq. ft. of flag replaced (by guess who?). And all during a short period after just having fallen over backwards on the rim of a lurking, malign flowerpot. A gardener's backbone must be made of stern stuff indeed.

I mention the parable of the flagstone and the backbone not in search of sympathy because gardeners live the most barbaric of lives without such luxury. No. Mention is made merely to reemphasize the point that the mind and the body must work together if ever anything is to be "gotten done" in the garden.

The mind does not, for example, remove stumps or stones . . . it only thinks it does. Hauling sand or gravel, soil, rocks, manure, timbers, bags of fertilizer or lime or peat moss, pots of soil, flats, balled shrubs—these are not brain-jobs. Removing and moving sod, digging flower beds, grading and leveling, turning and screening compost heaps—let the brain do these things and they will not be gotten done—I can assure you.

There are those sorts who might argue that such activities are not gardening after all, but rather some sort of pre-masochistic behavior requiring medical attention. Gardening to them concerns pulling weeds, mowing the lawn, planting, or watering. Or perhaps hiring people to do these things. Activities which, in my own garden at least, had so far taken up relatively little time because there was no garden in which to take them up.

I *was* planning the garden, but in so doing a great deal of stage machinery had to be put in place in preparation for the players. It would not do, after all, to set out all of the players on an empty platform and then try to fit the scenery snugly around them—an awkward task at best. The drudgery of production and direction was left to the bones while the brain was the thing wherein we would capture the spirit awaiting in the wings.

In actuality a great many bones must be cast about the gardening platform if one is to get the planning right before the major planting begins. Next to the gardener's own back, nothing else defines his garden so much as its own backbone.

The paths, for instance. Where will they go? What awaits the walker at the next turn? Will there be long vistas to take in at a glance or sharp turns which lead to private moments? Will the viewer walk on grass or stone, asphalt or concrete? Will there be a bench—say in that corner over there? Or a waterfall cascading alongside the path with perhaps a bridge crossing over at one point?

Where will the water taps be located? I soon grew tired of lugging watering cans all about the place as there was only the one tap at the back of the house. It would never do, for example, to build the terrace only to find that I'd have to remove parts of it to put in more taps. Which, of course, is exactly what I did (I mean I can't think of everything).

Structures! Where would the lath house eventually go? I had to know now, before I built it on top of the place where the water pipes were supposed to go (occasionally I actually do get something right). Trellises and pergolas could use some thought. Rock walls and fences were best placed where needed, preferably the first time!

And finally come a few actual "garden-type" thoughts such as where will the hedge be most effective or where will the pine be needed most in 20 years? Main plant structures such as beds, borders, shrubberies, backdrops, and divisions, need to be noted and some of the slow things can even be planted. Here it *is* necessary to place out a few players on the stage, for example slow-growing conifers, even though they might be lost for a while in the shuffle. These are backbones which may take ages to stiffen up and it is best not to wait too long before putting them in. Reason must prevail at times, even if we don't believe in it.

One does well to respect reason, all else considered, for in the end it is the gardener's "manual" backbone which ultimately achieves the effects for which we strive. It is the gardener's "mental" backbone that does the planning. But the two had better work together if the garden is ever to arise on a backbone of its own.

6
Paper Gardens I

PLOTS AND PLANS

Partly in defense of self, but largely out of laziness, I do a lot of my gardening on paper. It seems so much more reasonable to push a paper rock around than a real one, or to dig a paper hole, or to move a 20 ft. paper tree before it is too late.

I have no formal training in landscape design, which should be taken as a blessing of some sort, and most of what follows may be ignored if you wish. I do, however, have enough formal training in my own specialty to realize that "training" usually means one does things the way everyone else thinks they ought to be done . . . that is the way one is taught to do things. This is especially true for beginning experts who have yet to discover the differences between knowledge and fact.

The planning of my garden has been done without benefit of counsel, so to speak. There are those who upon viewing the results agree. I cannot help these people in the least, nor could I ever satisfy them unless I did things "their way." But a respectable garden is for the gardener first, you see, and regardless of the botch we make of it, it is our own darling little bastard and we shall love it. We may covet other gardens, even copying bits of them, but none of them will be "our" garden even if transplanted in their entirety to our own property. So it is best to get on with one's own thoughts and plans and let the garden be one's own . . . but prepare for the worst, for it will surely come.

Having made this cynical statement, I must now suggest that gardening does involve two factors (other than money and labor, of course—everything needs that), the two factors being thought and planning. Not textbook thoughts, mind you, but common-sense sorts—the most difficult sorts, to be absolutely candid.

It is not wise, we know, to plant a tree in the middle of the driveway. This confounds common sense. Yet we rarely lift an eyebrow when someone plants a beautiful, 6 ft. conifer on either side of the front door, even though we know each will grow only 60 ft. tall and 20 ft. wide. We have neither thought nor planned about what is going to happen to these trees, or more importantly to the entranceway and foundations, in time.

This is a gardener's duty, then, to think about what goes into the garden and to plan for the overall integration of the house, the plants, the pathways, the pipes, and the peculiarities. Well, not actually the peculiarities . . . you can't plan for these, they just seem to happen.

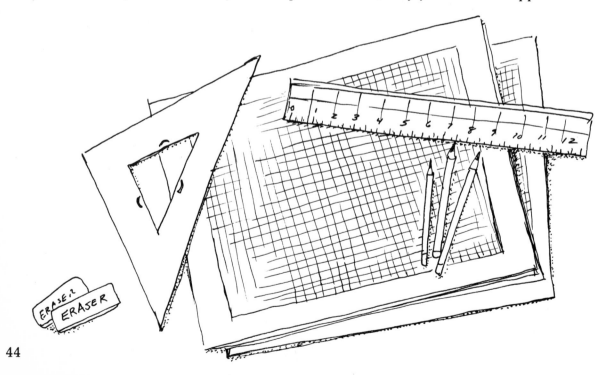

Plotting. I have, sitting before me, a fairly comprehensive article from a most respectable garden magazine, on the business of getting on with this planning business. The process, so says the article, is properly begun with paper and pencil, and I agree wholeheartedly. But after a few paragraphs the author begins to worry me a bit. We find that to plan a garden properly we must have architect's tracing paper, compass, triangle, scale ruler, architectural graph paper (in addition to drafting paper), felt-tip pens, line level, 100-ft. carpenter's tape, possibly a hand-sighting instrument, instant camera, soil samples, and a dozen other bits and pieces of stuff that seem only to get in the way. I am somewhat surprised that a suggestion wasn't made for a drafting table, loft study, and three dozen helpers to actually do the work.

One does not need these things in the least. What one truly needs are the following:

```
Graph paper . . . . . . . . . . . . . . . . . 1 sheet
Pencil. . . . . . . . . . . . . . . . . . . . 1 #2 lead
Erasers . . . . . . . . . . . . . . . . . 275 pounds
```

The above supplies have lasted me for six years and I've only just run out of erasers. It does pay to get the heavy-duty graph paper; mine is made of sheet metal, but something lighter is preferable, especially if you work on your lap as I frequently do (I damn near killed Bruno one night when the plan dropped on the floor). Really now, one needs nothing more than the bare essentials listed above and perhaps a tape measure.

In my own garden nothing much actually happened during the first year except, as I have pointed out, the introduction of the house to the garden and a feeble-minded attempt at growing vegetables for social acceptance. These two undertakings *and* the official mapping of the "estate" as it were. At that time the garden was easy to map because there was essentially nothing there.

I concentrated for the first few years on the rear yard which was a 100-ft. square with scarcely anything in it except lawn, two quite magnificent Japanese maples of some age, and a miscreant wisteria which wasn't certain if it wanted to be a standard rampant or a rampant standard. A dead walnut (or hickory) of some 20 ft. in height and a multi-trunked, decaying apple tree were both felled from the center of the square which opened up the yard completely.

After plotting in these few bits of vegetation on my map, I unfortunately had to contend with the peripheral trees which were somewhat more of a problem because they cast shade every which way. In the morning a north-south row of vegetation cast shade on the east side of the garden. I could do nothing with this shade as it was cast by the two Japanese maples, which I would not cut down, and a bunch of mulberry trees and a walnut tree which my neighbors would not let me cut down. This hardly seemed neighborly of them, but as the trees were on their side I was defeated.

On the west side of the square was another row of trees casting shade all afternoon. On my side of the fence, these trees included a stupendous specimen of our native tulip-poplar, another rather large apple tree, and a willow with terminal rickets (or, more precisely, rickety terminals). In addition, a charming fencerow had sprung up consisting of dogwood, sassifras, privet, raspberry, blackberry, multiflora rose, and smilax. Almost all this remains after five years, except the willow. A year or two after flailing some of its more rotten limbs it was severely severed, and the apple is about to go the same way. I had planted a shade garden in this area but soon the afternoon sun will come bounding in and then what? Planning can only take you so far, and it is often wise not to think *how far!*

The north side of the square was a simple matter, merely a silver maple about 20 ft. across and 50 ft. tall . . . on my side of the fence. A shade-caster of great dimension, undoubtedly equalled below ground by an insidious mass of roots which had a strangle hold on the lower portion of the garden. The south side of the square consisted of the house and a venerable old apple tree (both over two stories), both of which cast total shade. On any given sunny day, I reckoned, there might have been a 6-in. square of sunlight in my garden somewhere . . . I just never knew where.

My basic problem is, I suppose, that I just don't have the nerve to cut down trees without provocation. Fortunately for the garden's sake, the huge apple tree next to the house broke up and I had to have it removed. I could not have done it on my own; the silver maple attests to that, as it is still standing in spite of the fact that it is a horrid tree. Someday, I fervently hope, it shall fall over of its own accord. (I have introduced a colony of carpenter ants as a start.)

This plotting of the status quo is among the most important aspects, I feel, of gardening. It gives us an initial idea of how things appear, what established plants, if any, are worth saving, and what objectives one might work towards. In my case I had a nearly blank canvas upon which to work, but one which would have nearly ever-changing conditions of light during the course of a day, a season, or a year. After several years of wandering and watching, of measuring and plotting, it has become all too apparent that I have a garden of extremely complicated light patterns.

These problems of light and shadow, of heat and cold, have been among my most perplexing problems, and ones with which I still struggle. It seems that no sooner is one area analyzed and planted to a certain light condition, than a tree falls over, a shrub grows too tall, or the area has to be dug for a sewer line. But these "acts of gardening" will occur whether one plans correctly or not, so we may as well try to do it right to begin with. Eventually something will work . . . I think.

The basic thing about planning, I feel, is to determine what purpose the garden will serve. That, of course, is a matter for each of us to decide. Shall it be a show place for our botanical collections or a run for our doggie friends? A field for sport or a storage lot for used cars? An outdoor room for entertaining the masses or a temple for one? The choice is ours and will determine how we get on with things.

Parceling out the future. In my garden, I have worked toward realizing two basic objectives. One has been to add an outdoor area as an extension of my all-too-small house. The other, to develop a garden of retreat—a place to escape the cares of the outside world. Do not take me incorrectly, however, I do not mean I wished to live in a monastery, in reverential contemplation, shut off from the known world. No, I just wanted some place to regain my composure after commuting home from work.

This garden of composure would *have* to contain certain elements which I deemed essential to maintain sanity. There would have to be a rock garden and some water—perhaps a pond or two, or even a stream. I needed these things, artificial though they might have been, to ease my spirit into the natural world, far, far, from the commuting crowd. I needed vistas with no sign of inhumanity to let the eyes soar to infinity and relieve eyes, sore from peering through a microscope all day. I needed some secret places, small, snug, secure, where I could pretend the house really didn't need painting after all. I needed a garden of timelessness, where flowers viewed today could have been viewed as easily by Shakespeare or Parkinson. I needed shade gardens where I could retreat from the hellish summers, and sun gardens where I could retreat from the even more hellish remainder of the year. But probably what I needed most was to be placed in a home for the feeble-minded. I mean the garden *was* only 100 ft. square!

To attempt all of this properly demanded a staggering amount of plotting and planning, not to mention a great degree of lunacy and self-denial. I mean, one person could not achieve these goals all at once, although we gardeners usually are willing to give it a try. It would be necessary, I agreed with myself, to organize the main features of the garden on paper so that I might work out some sort of rational schedule to parcel out my efforts and to parcel out the future, so to speak.

I think gardeners do more of this parceling business than any other sort of person; we have to because we deal with living objects . . . objects that take time to develop, yet change constantly. No sooner is a seedling tree set in place than it is casting too much shade; a heather sprawling all out of proportion to its importance; a dianthus departs or a campanula collapses, leaving a worrisome, gaping hole in the rockery.

Somehow I had to parcel out the future so that I knew where things would go when their time came. If I had the paths on paper, or the secret places, or the rocks, then I could plan and plant around these invisible backbones until I eventually had the time to actually build such supporting garden structures.

To some this may sound a bit backward; I mean, to plant the garden and then put in the paths, the rocks, the pipes, and so forth. Most books would probably tell you to build everything first and then plant. I did not have the time to build paths or dig ponds or put in rocks. I did not have the money to purchase landscape-sized plants, nor did I know exactly how to make the paths. About all I could afford to purchase at the time was a spade, a fork, and some seeds, and then to "have at it."

With my paper plan, for example, I could mark off the pond and the shape of the garden around it, and then strategically place small, inexpensive evergreens which would be landscape-size (I hoped) by the time I finally got around to digging the pond. I could put small hedges and seedling specimen plants at their proper places in the scheme of things and hope eventually to cut out a path or build a wall around them.

Planning. I am still working with the original plan drawn up over seven years ago, and while many of the details have changed, to be certain, the goals are still much the same. I shall attempt to give a thumbnail sketch, or barebones treatment of the design. Frankly, descriptive garden writing leaves me cold, either to read or write it. But I suppose a little is necessary and I do it only in the interest of future walks down the garden path.

Right now there is painfully little by which to demonstrate that any of my plans will work, in spite of endless years of diligent labor. That is largely because every undertaking in the garden has been based upon removing the sod, improving the soil, fighting off the repeated invasions of unrequited weeds, growing and planting the desired plants, and then discovering that they are invariably in the wrong place. Experience may be a fine teacher, but I have been a painfully slow learner.

As you may recall (although this is no longer a certainty by any means) the garden behind the house was a nearly empty box of about 100 ft. square. I shall herewith save one thousand of those pearls of prose used by garden writers and illustrate my point:

Also I have already mentioned the vegetable bed and terrace, which in the beginning were merely penciled in about as follows:

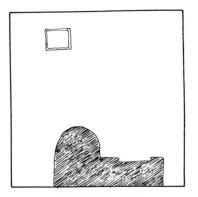

Next I must include the basic focal point of the garden . . . the point to which all eyes are immediately drawn . . . namely the silver maple which I had not the nerve to chop down:

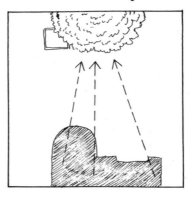

Nerve or not, I did not want this tree to be the focal point for reasons of geometry. It was the shortest distance from nearly any point in the garden, and I wanted to utilize the longest axis to achieve maximum vistas. In point of fact, then, I wanted the viewer to observe thusly, and this became the first principle of my garden design:

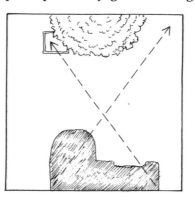

It must have a technical name, but I don't know what it is, I just call it the "longest distance between two points" principle.

The next stage in the design would appear to contradict this principle a bit, but it doesn't actually do so if given some reasonable corollaries. And we gardeners can be reasonable sorts (sometimes). I first read of this concept in a book by the well-known British author Beverley Nichols, an author for whom I have great admiration and to whom I shall return again. The principle states simply that a garden is doubled in size by being cut in half. Following this tenet rigorously might produce the following result if accepted without question:

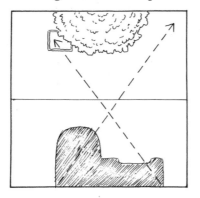

Somehow, however, this did not seem to be what I had in mind, and I eventually stumbled across the perfectly obvious notion that a garden could be halved any number of ways by merely rotating the halfway point. Thus the following possibility came into focus:

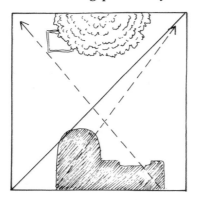

Now we were getting somewhere . . . I think. So far, everything had been laid out in stark, straight lines, but this was, after all, only a piece of paper with some bareboned thinking on it. That is what paper is for, actually. I could not have gotten half this far if I had been running out every three days to dig new holes and move plants all about the place until they "looked right." (Now that I *have* the plan I actually do this moving with impunity. It is a much better feeling to make mistakes when you know you've made plans for them than if you haven't. You may take my word on that.)

Getting from straight lines to the shape of a two-dimensional garden took a great deal of trial and error; actually mostly error, but that is what the erasers are for. Many a winter's evening was spent working and reworking my paper garden until it began to look something like this:

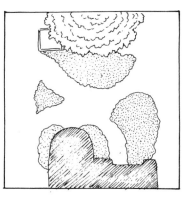

I maintained the diagonal vistas, such as they were. It did not take much additional planning to go the final step and fill in the peripheral areas as follows:

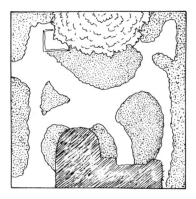

At this point, several things might be becoming quite clear to you, or vice versa. Firstly, things were starting to get complicated. That was okay with me, I needed lots of separate "spaces" as I've pointed out at the beginning of this ramble. Secondly, the lawn was disappearing at as rapid a rate as possible. That was okay with me, too, because that's the

52

way I planned it. I was trading quantity for quality . . . I hoped. Thirdly, all the lines and squiggles on the paper were creations of pencil, not plants. That was great with me, because the plants were growing there in my head somewhere, just waiting to be transplanted.

7
Paper Gardens II

PLANTS AND PLANS

Proportions. Having assembled the paper work, so to speak, and presuming we now have some plan, there is the not-so-trivial matter of what to plant. And here I can be of no use to anyone whatsoever. All I can say is it helps to have lots of books, nursery catalogs (if not taken too seriously), and thousands of trips to public and private gardens, garden centers, nurseries, and libraries. The basic problem here is that to use plants proficiently it helps to know what plants can do in the garden because they *are* the garden. It helps, but it is not critical.

I suppose there might be gardens that don't have plants, but it seems rather rude to call them such. A yard, for example, where a few ivy or pachysandra huddle forlornly between the fence and an Olympic-size swimming pool scarcely seems fit to be called a garden. And an idle scattering of fuschias around an outdoor grill could hardly be thought of as a triumph of the genre. Charitably these might be called decorations, perhaps, but not gardens.

Not that gardens need to be anything larger than a flower pot, a concrete trough, or even a half whisky barrel (if one is first permitted the common good sense to empty its contents). No, size is not the concern of definition.

Take, for example, the case of some friends who have cultivated

a small corner of a dusty, dingy alleyway in the center of an urban sprawl not 3 miles from the White House. This spot of land, not more than two parking spaces by urban standards, sandwiched between curbstone and apartment, is an oasis of undulating, multi-faceted texture which stops everyone who stumbles by. (If only those with dogs would be so kind as not to stop it would surely benefit us all.)

The truly amazing thing, I find, is that this little scrap of land . . . with its colorful naturalness, its occasional tire track or two, its puddle of oil from a thoughtless crank, its visits by unhousebroken dog owners . . . this scrap of land is not even owned by its caretakers. It was adopted into the family, so to speak, and is nurtured with as much care as if it *were* the caretakers' own garden.

Our affinity with plants need not be particularly learned or pedantic . . . we need not know the names, or heights, or shapes, or even colors. In fact, we need think scarcely anything about plants at all if the truth be known. They've been around quite some time without our help and they've done remarkably well without it. All we need do to verify this, many of us at least, is to look back a few years at the gardens our grandmothers might have made.

I know little of my grandmother, which is just as well for you, except that she was born in 1876, crossed the plains as a girl, was settled in Missouri for awhile and then again in Nebraska. Here, towards the end of her life and the beginning of mine, we met. She lived in a wisp of a house, clapboard and tar shingles, no car and no plumbing to speak of. The only things we had in common were our sizes, our ages, and our gardens. Though mine was but a few nasturtiums grown from seed, hers seemed like acres to a small, city child who had known only apartment dwelling.

She was always a gardener, this diminutive, bent grandma, at least according to my mother who had known her quite well. Mostly a survivalist by necessity, not by fashion. But there were always flowers around, and I was lucky to see a true grandma's garden during the rare times I visited her. Would that my memory could serve better, for I cannot remember all the plants therein, but I can remember the effect as I used to prowl through the underbrush.

The garden was one mostly of chance, by this time in her life— West Nebraska sandhill, contained (sort of) by railroad ties which my grandfather probably borrowed from the nearby tracks where he had worked. A huge windmill and storage tank provided all the water for the place and overshadowed a corner of the garden.

This garden contained some order, I am certain, but it was not apparent. There were rows of vegetables and some strawberries, but as I recall everything was so overgrown with flowers it was no simple task to harvest supper. I truthfully recall only a total abandon of what I later learned were sweet williams, cosmos, and hollyhocks (the plain and single ones which one nearly has to kill for these days). And there were red-hot pokers, a plant with which I curiously have no rapport.

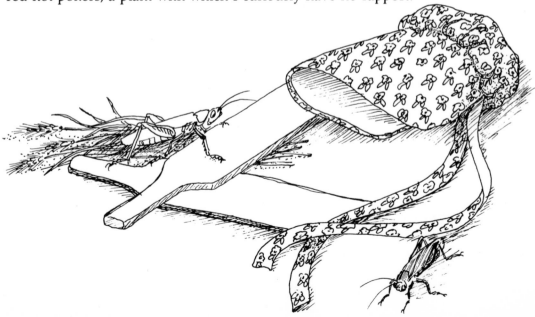

Most of the flowers were annuals (or biennials) which reseeded themselves every year wherever they took a fancy. They were on their own for life and planning, and they did quite well, thank-you, without help from anyone. Anyone, that is, except my grandmother who would go out in her sunbonnet, pick up the two wooden paddles, and smack the hell out of those pesky grasshoppers.

The point of this little story is that flowers, at least the smaller sorts, can and do take care of themselves just as if they were weeds. However, most of us have grown not to accept randomization of plants as a garden, and we are not happy in our more structured urban existence to let flowers have their say. Perhaps we have some things yet to learn.

Dimensions. If we are unwilling to let flowers manage for themselves then the alternative seems to be planning their lives for them. And this is where paper comes in handy. Without too much trouble, or too much talent, we can dash off little sketches of how things might look if everything went right (a highly suspicious notion). We can take our master plan and make a bird's-eye view of how junipers might sprawl out across a bank and over the paths, or how a pine might overshadow the house, or a red maple the pond. On a smaller scale we might visualize dianthus nestling up to a rock or attacking a campanula, perhaps heather tumbling between a crevice, or even waterlilies on the water.

These are our horizontal dimensions, and they are, perhaps, a bit difficult to comprehend from above. But another plan, this one for vertical effects, may be sketched if you are unfortunately like I am . . . an obsessive compulsive. The affect of this drawing is to render the cat's-eye view of things, which is more nearly our own manner of observation. Here we can plot in the height of the fastigate Scotch pine compared, for example, to that of the buddleia next to it. We can also figure sidewise spreads as well, but only up to a point. And I think we've reached it.

There is, after all, only so much that can be done on paper, and eventually we must strike off on a more direct pathway to the garden. But it is difficult, I believe, to know what this way is unless we have first done a little planning, a little paper work. In my own style of paper gardening, I try to work out the designs, the heights, the spread, the colors, and the seasonality of the garden before I actually do any planting, because pushing a pencil around is a lot easier than pushing dirt. Also, it is possible to garden all year long with this approach.

Nothing could possibly make this point better than a night such as this one. It is a January evening, cold, dark and heavy. Rain has fallen all day, but is now turning to slush. The wind whips from the north and splatters the side of the house with noise. Soon, says the forecaster, the slush will turn to snow and ice—just in time for morning's commute. The pond sits just beyond the French doors, frozen over since time began, it seems. And Bruno lies unmoved in lugubrious slumber for lo these past many hours.

Just the right sort of night to gently unfurl our garden plans, to feel summer's warmth surge through those frozen, tight old sinews, to build another rock wall—perhaps over there, along the vista-walk; or to plot out that new bed of daffodils and daylilies.

But if all of this should seem a bit too structured or a tad too stale, perhaps you might prefer another system which I use. Just plant out what you wish and draw up the plans when you've got the garden as you wish it to look. This is really the most efficient way, and it makes other gardeners think you are terribly organized. I won't tell, if you don't.

8
Musical Manure,
Or a Matter of Piles

I once even saw my driveway—it was the day I moved into the house. As I recall, it was a blackish gray sort of asphalt-type affair . . . the drive, that is, not the house. There might have been a few cracks; it has, after all, been awhile.

For many years now, this drive has been out of view, camouflaged as various sorts of piles of things. For a very long period it was rocks awaiting their place in the garden. And then came gravel, followed by sand and gravel, followed by gravel and sand and horse manure.

Strangers would pull their car up to the front of the house, inspect the merchandise, and then ask if I delivered. Most of the time, though, the drive was so cluttered they could not find a place to park so they just drove on. This certainly has its advantages, and I recommend a certain air of clutter just to warn your friends or relatives not to stop by too often.

Unfortunately these piles of things, which have covered the drive since time began, confirm the frequent problem in my garden which results from *The Axiom.* Well, actually it is as close to an axiom as I care to get—namely:

Nothing in the garden is ever placed correctly the first time regardless of how well planned.

The corollary may be added:

The heavier an object is, the larger the choice of incorrect places it will be placed.

In the case of plants these moves are generally fairly simple. I consider herbaceous perennials, bulbs, alpines and even small shrubs to be OMFC (one-move-for-certain) items. Whereas larger shrubs and trees (including ever bigger rootballs) generally require two or three displacements to find the suitably correct position. Unhappily, I tend to permanently distress even the most vigorous of plants on about the third move.

Piles of flagstone, rocks, sand, or gravel, of course, have obvious implications for every imaginable form of strain, sprain, or back disorder. Never content to move one ton of sand once, for example, I generally manage to move it at least as many times as it takes to temporarily invalid myself.

Let us start these moves with the one commodity, however, which neither suffers of itself nor causes me to suffer in the many moves which must be made before its correct destiny is found. Manure! Particularly manure fresh from the source.

I am fortunate, though some might disagree, to live near a horse stable where gleanings are free for the taking. I am *doubly* fortunate to have a friend who has a truck and actually enjoys hauling the stuff to almost anyone who wants it (more of this knight in shining armor in another chapter). It is at this point that my personal fortunes end. From here on out it is musical manure for me.

The first stop in the game is at my driveway. It is here that the truckloads are dropped, always off-center, falling either on the lawn, the rock pile (twice-moved already to allow the truck to back down the drive), or the sand pile (ditto the rock pile). Ten cubic yards of fresh, steaming, heaven-sent horse manure. One could scarcely ask for more. One could ask, however, that it not be dropped on top of everything else. But, of course, one does not ask this too loudly under the circumstances.

The second move of the game now commences. Quickly, before the lawn is smothered (usually *after,* the way I play), one must move the spill over from its surface. The easiest move is to flip it back onto the pile in the drive. This seemingly saves a lot of time because one doesn't have to move it too far. Just a couple of feet. And so it begins.

A related optional play, and one I too frequently pursue, is the sudden need for a cartload of rock or sand. This requires moving the quantity of manure which has inevitably fallen just where it shouldn't. An even more tricky, but ever-so-skillful play, if one is up to it, is to be forced to move the manure so that one can get at the gravel in order to move the gravel so that one may get at the sand. I do this a lot. It is what I call the "last-most principle," that is, whatever is first-most in priority is last-most in reachability.

Ever intent on improving my skill at musical manure, I move from the simple spill over plays to the more strenuous relay races. This involves being forced to move the whole 10 cu. yd. as quickly as possible because someone actually wants to park in the driveway. Rather thoughtless, I think, after all garages are for parking; driveways are for better things.

Anyway, 31 cartloads and 2 miles later, I have completely cleaned off the drive, having placed the manure in the most remote area of the garden, namely the compost pile, where it will be incorporated at a later date. At least that is the principle.

It never *is* incorporated, of course, because it is needed immediately at some other currently expectant spot such as the nursery bed, the shrubbery, or the annual border. By this time, generally after three moves, the manure has found its final resting spot and is, in fact, nearly totally decomposed.

Actually, it is amazing how little remains of rotted manure. Not that I've made much of a study, mind you, but I have been incorporating truckloads of manure in certain beds now for some 4–5 years and it disappears as soon as it hits the ground. Why is it then, that a pile on the driveway sits forever? (Have you ever noticed that science never tackles these really tough questions?)

Sand and gravel are just like manure except heavier. They differ only in expense, and regardless of how enormous the sum of money spent, or how large the piles might start out, or how many hundreds of cartloads are moved, there is never enough in reserve to do half of the jobs necessary. True, it never rots like manure—or at least I think it doesn't—and it sits on the drive in massive quantities like manure. Yet, in the end it seems as if the entire 10 tons, taken cartload by endless cartload, can fill or level only the tiniest of a garden's vacant spots.

This matter of estimating quantities of material is one of the irksome factors which leads to so many piles in my garden. For even with my paper plans, my measurements, and my calculator, I am always off by just the amount it takes to keep my driveway perpetually covered in work.

Take gravel, for instance. By the time I near the end of my driveway reserve, I realize I have miscalculated by about a ton or two. The gravel path could be finished, I now realize, if *only* I had enough to cover five more feet. But for the delivery price of one ton of gravel one could purchase four tons so it just seems more economical to order the minimum amount that is delivered for free. More economical, perhaps, but not quite rational it would seem as the truck backs down the lane with 10 tons of gravel which will soon be splattered over the entire drive.

So now I cart gravel for weeks on end to finish off the pathway. To no one's surprise except mine, I discover, that it only takes a half ton of material—only 9½ tons remain resting on the drive. I think my calculator needs a new battery.

I consult my plans again to see if maybe there is some place in the garden that needs a little padding—say 9½ tons worth. There isn't. But actually, I discover, I could extend the path another 10 ft. or so, and that would take up at least another ton based upon the 5 ft. section I had just finished. This was obviously not the solution to the entire problem, but it seemed like a start.

After some weeks of hauling I discover to my dismay that 2 ft. short of my 10-ft. extended pathway I have run out of gravel. I cannot explain this exactly; perhaps I need a new calculator. Obviously at this point I should have ended the path 2 ft. short. But I discovered a need for additional gravel to redo a part of the terrace which was unexpectedly misbehaving.

Five years and 20 tons of gravel later, the predicament has not changed appreciably—the driveway is still covered. Sometimes I wish the garden would make up its mind, exactly, as to just what it is doing.

One of the more persistent problems I've had with piles, in the garden that is, is the accommodation of great quantities of soil and sod created by my compulsive excavations. As you may recall, nearly the entire garden was sod when I began my garden-making, which meant that almost any plan requiring change (which was any plan at all) produced endless piles of sod and soil.

With my paper plans I assumed I knew exactly what to do with this material, which has proved exactly wrong. Plans, I feel, can give a false sense of security—somewhat as if one actually *knew* what one were doing. This is a dangerously misleading conception.

The construction of the terrace, for example, required a great amount of excavation. First I had to uproot and crush a 100-sq.-ft.

65

concrete pad. This was broken into fist-size chunks with a sledge and was used in part as drainage backfill for the terrace. A pile of the larger pieces, however, still is moved from time to time until I can find some use for them.

Next came removal of the sod, about 800 sq. ft. Some was moved to the front garden to patch low spots near the lane, but the remainder began to pile up at an alarming rate along the fencerow at the eastern edge of the garden.

Then, too, came a great amount of soil which needed removal so that I might replace it with gravel and sand for drainage. This was piled on top of the removed sod until further notice. By this time it was beginning to look somewhat as if I were preparing to defend my eastern flank from the invading hordes. I was, actually. Earlier I had discovered that rain water cascaded down from my neighbor's acre and across my garden—creating a regular flood with every thunderstorm. A berm, I reasoned, would divert water towards the lower end of the property. It would also give me a place to store additional soil until I knew what to do with it.

The berm has performed its duty, surprisingly, and the extra soil also serves its purpose by waiting patiently in repose. I frequently borrow from it to build up some low spot (usually where I had taken too much soil away to start with), to fill flower pots or tubs, to backfill behind some stone wall, or to build up some great mound or other which I have decided to create (usually in the wrong place).

A great quantity of soil has moved about in my garden, and will be moved about again I am certain. And all by hand. I sometimes wonder if man hasn't inherited a propensity for earth moving, whether by hand or machine, from some lowly mole or other.

During my movements of various piles of things you might assume that I could learn one or two valuable lessons. Well, one perhaps, but certainly never two—that *is* expecting too much. I have actually learned one thing that has helped stay the endless tide of shifting piles, and it is what I call "composting in place." It is a cross between sheet composting and composting in a hidden compost pile (or bin) as we are normally taught. It is the only instance I can recall in which I may save myself a few unneeded moves.

From my paper plans I ascertain where I might conceivably want to mound soil and leave it. A future walled area, perhaps, or an elevated spot to grow azaleas, or a rise with which to break the flatness of my landscape. At this spot I begin to layer all the normal things one layers: a few dozen pieces of cut sod from a newly graveled pathway, shovelfuls of heavy clay from a drainage channel, leaves and branches from the newly graveled pathway, used kitty litter, weeds pulled from the newly graveled pathway, cut grass from my neighbor's lawn, cat litter from the newly graveled pathway, botanical refuse from the kitchen, and dead cats found misbehaving on the newly graveled pathway.

These things are piled and composted for several years, and I freely admit it is not exactly a pretty sight. Especially in the middle of the garden. But I've learned to take the bad with the bad and I just ignore it. What can you expect at a construction site, anyway? Eventually it will be a garden and that seems soon enough to me. And I don't have to move everything three times when I do it this way. Except, of course, when I discover I have to move the entire pile because it's in the wrong place. I've learned to expect that by now.

After manure and sand, gravel and sod, soil and compost, nothing much is left except for the rocks and flagstones. And for any-one's information, moving 5 cu. yds. of hot, steaming manure is far easier than moving even one rock—especially if it is heavy enough. That is basically because you can put a handle on manure in the shape of a pitchfork, spading fork, or shovel, but you can't find any handles on a rock no matter what shape it is.

With rocks, I have found, it is always best to set them correctly the first time . . . I have found this out because I never do. Rocks are no different in principle than gravel—which is just little tiny rocks—or than sand—which is just little tiny gravel. It is only logical, then, that all three should be treated the same. Yet somehow the results of misplacing 300 pounds of gravel is never quite the same as misplacing a 300-pound rock. I should know because I once put such a rock in the wrong place and had to move it.

This rock was the bridge stone for a pond I had dug. It took several days of maneuvering, pain, and cursing to move this rock on a platform and some rollers that I had contrived. The rock had to move only about 50 ft. which was easy enough. But then I had to position it over the water with each end resting on the bank on either side. I'm not certain how I managed to do this, especially as I did not use a hoist, but I did and eventually paid the price with a pinched nerve in my neck.

The next year, however, after overwintering in place, the banks supporting the ends of the rock began to collapse and the rock began sinking into the water. There was nothing to do but remove the rock, dig out both banks, and put in some construction blocks for support. This accomplished, I went back to the doctor.

I figure that all of the rocks in my garden (6 tons to date) have been moved at least twice and some have been moved as many as five or six times. One time they'll be moved to make room for the manure, another to make room for the sewer, yet again for the construction of the stone wall, but then they'll be in the way of the pond, and on and on they move. My stones rarely gather any moss—that's for certain.

And here I am, now, making plans for next year's new rock garden and wall. The plans call for 20 tons of rock. Now let's see, if I move those twice that's 40 tons, and if I move them three and half times that's 70, and if I move them four and three-quarters times that's . . . that's . . . but wait!

I think it's best that you move on to the next chapter while I run and get my calculator. I'd best check my health insurance, too, so I'll probably be a while.

9
Potting up the Pathway

I was sitting on the path, working across the gravel, when I spied a rather odd-looking sort of thing in a nearby *Chaemecyparis* . . . a pulsating mass of some sort. Not exactly the normal thing one expects from a plant, but upon close inspection it proved to be only a swarm of bees and nothing sinister in the least. As my next-door neighbor keeps bees I began walking briskly towards the lane to see if he might have been missing something when a ringing telephone cut me short. I dashed back down the drive, hurled the porch steps two at a time, and rushed to pick up the phone.

"Yes," I asked rather expectantly as I was anticipating a call of some magnitude.

"We're conducting a survey," came the reply, "on shopping."

"I'm sorry," I said breathlessly, and without too much thought, added, "I'm busy potting up the pathway."

What the caller might have made of this I shall never know, as I hung up rather rudely. I do not like telephone solicitations, especially when I'm in the middle of a bee swarm.

Because the bees are irrelevant for the remainder of this story, I shall say no more except that they left. As for paths, however, so much has already been written by others that I may safely write what I wish with the confidence that no one will listen anyway. And if they did, nothing would change their minds in the least. It doesn't mine.

I grew up in gardens which had no paths. I don't know if this is particularly good or bad, but it is true. I do not feel that I suffered much from the experience. The gardens which surrounded the houses of my childhood were composed largely of small islands of land which lay between patio and fence, patio and house, driveway and fence, or lawn and house. One either walked on the concrete or on the lawn; life was simple in those days. A few strategically placed stepping stones always gave my small feet just enough feeling of instability to add danger to any garden romp. At a more reasonable age, however, such steps serve merely to impress upon one the size of one's own foot and how easily it might be twisted.

My next exposure to paths was of a totally different and much more substantial nature. At the age of 15 I became willingly indentured to a garden of just over one acre. It was a hilltop garden which extended down to the "flat" (as the base of the hill was known) and was crisscrossed with what seemed like miles of asphalt walks. For nearly a decade I trudged those paths dragging hoses from rhododendron to azalea, from iris to dahlia, and from rock garden to lathhouse. Uncounted miles were trod on those ways, tons of weeds were carted from garden to compost, gallons of new plants wound from nursery and lathhouse to garden, and all the while its owners cultivated the poor soil that was mine. I have never been fond of asphalt as an entity unto itself, but it is now too much a part of my sole to ever be forgotten.

Since childhood days I have walked on just about every kind of path imaginable and all have their good points as well as bad. My own pathways are still in a state of consolidation so that what I have to say about them is not set in concrete, so to speak. I am always looking for the perfect pathing material . . . that is, one I can afford . . . and the ones I have settled upon might be considered altogether cheap by some, but are labor expensive by anyone's account. They will not suit everyone's taste, and even I grow weary of the maintenance on occasion, but they are still my favorite materials in spite, even, of the cost.

PATHS OF GRASS

If it were not for the fact that grass grows so awfully fast it would be about my favorite paving material. This is especially true in my garden because the entire area was grass to begin with. It has been merely too easy to lay out the paths as I imagine they should be, and then simply to cut out the garden from around them. The initial cost is reasonable, I suppose, being primarily the price of a good spade and an industrial-strength truss. But, although the process is simplicity itself, it is not without its problems as my back is constantly reminding me.

Now, if one wished to take schooling in how a proper grass walk is made, the correct thing to do would be to visit an English garden. Unfortunately, having seen such walks, it has become more difficult to live with my own. The only solution, of course, is to accept the English examples as illusions of what might be possible if one but lived in a cold, wet miserable climate where everything grew pathetically wonderfully. Where lawns were tightly packed emerald green carpets of perfectly parallel blades, and one might expect a small white ball to roll past one's foot at any moment.

Some gardens, reluctantly, are founded upon a premise of reality, and mine is one of them. Therefore, I accept my lumpy, dandelion-infested, sometimes-even-green areas as somewhat reasonable facsimiles of lawn, at least in name. It is the best I can do for the moment, but it does make for certain problems when it comes to pathways.

Take, for example, the ground ivy . . . please! No matter how much back-breaking effort is put into its extermination, there are always half-a-dozen strands running off the path into the borders. This has about as much appeal, naturally, as someone smiling while a piece of spinach dangles between his front teeth. Regardless of how nice the garden (or the person) might otherwise appear, the viewer becomes preoccupied more by life's slight distraction than by the gardener's intended focal point.

Obvious optical disappointments aside, the pathways which I have constructed constitute a slightly more devious challenge than merely keeping their edges in bound. The walks serve as a seed bank for all sorts of nasty little things that sooner or later wander off into the beds: dandelions with decisiveness, plantains with pervasiveness, sorrel with certainty, and violets with vengeance.

Practicality notwithstanding, grass for walks seems to be about the most natural of all paving materials, and its use can scarcely be faulted when compared with, for example, concrete. Yet, because of this fact, I think grass is not the best of all choices to serve exclusively as a pathway for the garden. That is to say, a garden is not generally a natural object anyway, and attempts to integrate pathway materials too carefully may result in a visitor's use of primroses as stepping stones. Better, perhaps, a shade of artificiality for balance than too much of a good thing.

AND OF GRAVEL

It has been said of gravel that it was once "the most popular of all surfacing materials" (Arthur Hellyer, 1976, *The Collinridge Encyclopedia of Gardening*), and that its use "is absurd" (Henry Mitchell, 1981, *The Essential Earthman*). Who is one to believe? In matters of such disparity, I usually choose to believe myself, and you might as well do the same (believe yourself, that is). It is all a matter of taste, you see, this gardening thing. Taste modified by cash, but none-the-less, taste. In my garden, for example, I should like to have expansive pathways of flagstone combined with granite-lined borders. I should also like to eat . . . and the two are not entirely compatible. So I compromise, which is really the basic law of the garden.

On the surface, so to speak, gravel would seem to have its bad points and its good ones as any proper compromise ought to. But actually when thoroughly studied, gravel paths might prove to be an exception to the art of compromise, as well as a veritable gold mine of thrift. Of course some of these benefits are for the soul as well, and these make the choice even better. I shall attempt to prove my point.

Opponents of gravel are quick to point out the various "problems" which they apparently find insurmountable and unsupportable. Such things as inability to stand hard wear, the necessity of rolling and tamping, the raking, weeding, and so forth. No one mentions, however, the worst part of making any path, namely the endless preparation required. As far as I am concerned, once the excavation for the path is finished, any other work is merely gratuitous. (Incidentally, that is one added plus for a grass pathway . . . no excavation if the sod is in place.)

Let us assume, for a moment, that we have laid out our pathway and we are about to begin the great task of excavation. We must have some place to move the excavatee, as it were. This is where our paper garden comes in handy, for we can begin the process of mound building, surface restructuring, and backbreaking at this point. Or alternatively, lacking a specific site, we may appropriate an out-of-the-way corner such as the compost pile, behind the garden shed, or the driveway. It cannot be overstressed at this point, however, that no matter where you place this material there will be too much of it and it will be in the wrong place. This is just a law of gardening and there is nothing you nor I can do about it.

Although excavation is painful on occasion, at least one ends up with mounds of usually good topsoil which may be used elsewhere in the garden for any number of purposes. This is an advantage if you have a relatively flat, dull expanse of space upon which you might wish to create some relief. (Such as my garden.) Whatever the purpose to which you put this soil, it would have to be dug for any sort of path so we may dismiss the most difficult aspect of path-making at this point.

After we have excavated and constructed our gravel path (the details of which I leave to those all-too-numerous "how-to" books), we must now brace ourselves for one of *the* endless tasks of which the experts speak: the tamping and rolling patrol. If one uses loose, rounded gravel of the "pea" or stream-bed sort, I suppose this tamping business might become never-ending. Every foot that treads the path would kick foot-fulls into the garden and every child would instinctively pelt fistfuls at the cat or into the pond. The most obvious solution to this problem is not to let humans (or children) use the paths. This seems perfectly civilized to me, yet few will listen. The less obvious solution to the problem is to use crushed stone, preferably bluestone, which is both angular and more or less coated with a fine dust which acts as a cementing agent. Not only do the paths stay relatively firm following light initial tamping, but the countless trips you make back and forth from the compost pile to the weed pile (i.e, the garden) will do all of the rolling and tamping that needs be done. It is all too simple.

As to the problem of raking, I have never given it a second thought. Paths need to be raked, whether they are cement, macadam, asphalt, or marbles. I see not the problem therein. As a matter of fact, one of the most enjoyable of all garden tasks to my mind is the raking of the paths. There are those who revel in the brutish feats of the garden— the digging, hauling, or building . . . not I. That stuff must be done, of course, and I do it as my disintegrating back will allow. But I am more capable of the "tidying" sorts of tasks, I suppose, and I enjoy them more.

To rescue a weed-choked flower bed or to clean a leaf-strewn path . . . now that *is* a pleasure. To listen as tines of leaf rake sing in vibrating harmony over a path's varying surface; bamboo rakes like so many muffled shakuhachi in the distance; metal tines ringing evermore-highly spirited with changing texture. To hear the whisper of the sole as it crunches softly along a gravel walk could be our own lot in life if we do not take too seriously what others might write. If ever I should have to serve the ethers in perpetuity, I would like to be the fellow who rakes the gravel at a Zen temple. That's not asking too much of life, is it!

In addition to the rather personal benefits of raking gravel, there is always the straight-forward aspect of definition in the garden. Not that gravel acts so much as a dictionary, but rather it lets one know that primroses are not, after all, stepping stones. It separates the garden from the ground, so to speak, and makes us aware that one should not go wandering off into the bush without an invitation. And that is precisely what a path should be . . . an invitation to explore, and it should be arranged in the garden so that one need not trample to achieve the result.

And now to the final, yet seemingly worst problem of the gravel walk . . . weeds. As several gardening texts point out, weeds in gravel paths may be taken care of by use of weed-killers. This, to me, is abhorrent, and it does not work particularly well as I have found out on numerous occasions. I've tried preemergence, prophylactic treatments to no seeming avail, and a few spot applications of the newest "wonderkiller" which does work on a limited basis (say a particularly "dandy lion" of leonine proportions). But these are, I am now convinced, the wrong approach to the problem. The approach should be tolerance and a redefinition of the term "weed."

As you may recall, at the beginning of this epistle, I warded off a telephone caller with the admonition that I was "potting up the pathway." And this was no idle nonsense. The previous year I had planted out seedlings of the Korean chrysanthemum which bloom in the first year. They had gone to seed in the fall and were now coming up in great profusion in the pathway. Never one to carp about proper excess, I went out with market packs in hand and transplanted nearly 6 dozen remarkably sturdy young plants. Not having the necessary stamina to callously uproot the remainder of these weedlings, I left them in place. The path became hopelessly overgrown, of course, but a weed by any other name might still be a chrysanthemum . . . and who am I to decide these things.

Since my experience with the chrysanthemums I have also potted up several species of dianthus, a linum, a potentilla, and an arenaria or two. And who's to say that this might not even be the best method of growing and propagating one's garden?

A recent article entitled "The Gravel Path" by H. E. Bawden (Bulletin of the Alpine Garden Society, vol. 51, June 1983) speaks perfectly to this point. Mr. Bawden is the owner of a 10-ft.-wide gravel path of "considerable length." After experiencing difficulty with weeds for sometime, Mr. Bawden worked out a particularly effective solution. First, 2-ft. square, staggered slabs were laid up the middle for walking, and then, on the principal that if weeds could grow so could real plants, Mr. Bawden decided to save weeding labor "by covering the remaining gravel with plants." This he did propitiously with excess divisions and cuttings from the rock garden, aided by seedlings thrown in naturally from the sidelines—*Cyclamen, Erinus,* geraniums, *Tanacetum,* and even chrysanthemum (although in his case it was *C. weyrichii* and not the Korean mum as in mine). In some cases Mr. Bawden found that

75

normally encroaching plants were noticeably less invasive in the leaner gravel of the path than in good soil. With other plants, such as dusty miller, there was no reduction in "exuberance." Regardless of the thrift of these gravel-path plants, Mr. Bawden had "no failures" and the result was "labour-saving, with plants where weeds might have been."

I have tried to present a somewhat balanced appreciation for the gravel path as a framework of integrity within the garden; a structure which serves both to define that which outlines it and which confines those who tread upon it. But again, we are faced with a matter of taste. If you are the sort of person, for example, who walks down the garden path barefoot as Eleanor Perenyi does (*Green Thoughts*, Random House, 1981), then you may find gravel too "beastly" to walk upon. Fortunately, I wear shoes, but if I didn't, the presence of my unclad feet upon the path certainly would help to keep the weeds down.

10
Amongst the Rupturewort

There is a short pathway from my drive to the side porch which originally consisted of mud decorated with slate tripping stones. It was not a particularly effective approach to the house unless, of course, you enjoy falling in the mud.

To effect a rapid cure for this mud I planted a trailing, prostrate plant known as rupturewort. Its planting was actually more an offering to the ethers than establishment of a cure—but one can take nothing for granted in the garden. It is often better to err on the side of superstitious caution than to be painfully sorry.

Rupturewort is a weedy little plant having scarcely anything to recommend it other than its iron-like constitution as a floral footpath and, of course, its name. But it is not really the rupturewort to which I direct your attention, but rather the weeds that grow amongst it. They are what take my fancy.

Not that I enjoy weeds, mind you, for they really can be a damnable nuisance. But they do offer two rewards in return for their usually slight provocations. One is solitude because no one ever offers to help, and the other is thought because weeding is such a mindless chore.

The most basic thought one must address when weeding is certainly the obvious question "what is a weed?" If we do not think this through immediately and precisely we will have pulled out all of the plants that sit before us. In some gardens this might be classified as a virtue, but certainly not in ours. As I mentioned only a chapter ago, one gardener's weedy pathway is another's nursery bed. Weeds are not defined by the space involved but rather by the circumstances.

Amongst my rupturewort path sprout numerous plants, all of which initially must be called weeds. Most of these weeds are pulled and discarded but some are not. Take for instance the platycodons and dwarf marigolds that self-seeded from last year. They are removed and used elsewhere. Amongst the rupturewort they are weeds—transplanted they are not. All well and good.

But what of the Shasta daisies that have self-seeded? I remove part and replant them; I remove the excess and throw them away. What, then, are they? And what, even, of the rupturewort itself? Here the principal plant of the path has overgrown its boundaries and splashes willfully back into the Shasta daisies that border them. Now they are the weed—unless of course I transplant them as I do the platycodons and marigolds.

Obviously there is no simple definition of a weed even when we accept the simplest—a plant growing where the gardener does not want it. As with much of gardening, though, we need not ponder the problem too long. By trusting in our instincts and simply pulling, the problem of weeding becomes rather quickly a matter of hand-eye coordination controlled automatically by our brain. We do not need to think about it after the first few dandelions are dug.

In reality most of gardening is like weeding—mindless drivel— at least for those of us who do our own work. Digging holes, watering, mowing the lawn, nipping the chrysanthemums, strangling the cat . . . all rather prosaic things, really, scarcely needing any thought at all. (And rarely receiving any by the look of most gardens.) They get done because they need to get done.

One of the primary thoughts which might arise while weeding (or any other garden chore, for that matter) is not a very useful one really. But it always seems to arise, and I mention it here for the record. This is the thought that one should really be doing something else in the garden. Everything else, in fact.

If I am weeding, for example, my first reactionary thoughts are that I should be mowing the lawn, or watering, or transplanting seedlings. If I am mowing the lawn, I think about turning the compost heap, restructuring the terrace, or finishing my stone wall. If I am transplanting, my initial thoughts lie with trimming the wisteria, cutting back the dianthus, or even weeding. This gardening stuff is all a vicious cycle in case you hadn't noticed.

Sometimes I will jump up from what I am doing and rush to some other "more urgent" job that I suddenly realize needs immediate attention. Sometimes I do this four or five times in a row and get nothing done all day. This might even be considered a good day by some!

On other occasions I have attempted to double up on chores to avoid these thought problems, but I have relatively little skill at it. One can clear leaves and mow the lawn simultaneously, or perhaps weed and water at the same time, but that is about all. Even this really doesn't work because two jobs on the mind just reminds one more than ever that one should be doing yet another task somewhere. Straightly put, there is always one more job to do than a gardener has time to do it. I believe there is some innate, built-in timer which helps us regulate all of this work flow, so I often acquiesce and do what seems "right." "Go with the flow" is my motto.

Once the secondary work-alert alarm has ended—that is after we have finally settled upon the work to be done and we are actually calmly doing it with little or no thought of "urgent elsewheres"—then we might go into the next phase of mental exercises which I call "stream of unconscious" thought. In this mode topics arise, are discussed mentally, then are replaced in rapid succession by others.

There is no order to most of this thought; I mean it does not follow any prescribed pattern such as sleep supposedly does. Also this process is fairly personal in individual detail I am certain, but probably all of us have about the same sorts of thoughts. We work our way up in emotional distress from problems of home to office to government, wondering, for example, if we'll ever get dinner fixed for six guests on Thursday night, or if we can afford a new wiper blade for the car. Or why are our bosses so incredibly stupid? How can we get anything done at work with so many mindless interruptions? Or how can everyone else be so inefficient, ineffective, and wasteful? Eventually we will be working over in our minds new policies for national security, control of the world's population, the exact time to launch a preemptive nuclear strike, or possibly even something important such as whether to plant summer *or* winter squash. (We generally have answers to all of these questions, too, except of course for the squash.)

Why these thoughts arise might provide a good thesis topic for some poor graduate student. Perhaps the mind simply presents us with these minor problems so as to overcome the really serious aspects of the work at hand. Perhaps the weighty problem of how to extricate a dandelion from between two Shasta daisies is more than the mind can really handle. Or it may be that the sight of two madly wriggling worms where moments before there had been but one might be too much to bear. Whatever the correct explanation our mind seems to protect us relatively reasonably from our own selves.

Occasionally, all of this subterraneous rumination may result in a useful thought or two, but mostly it just results in ulcers. After one has sorted out and solved most of the world's greater problems (while still weeding out the oxalis, of course), there comes a period of inner calm known technically as "the inner calm period." During this respite— lasting perhaps 30–40 seconds—a great moment of inspiration may erupt. Nine times out of ten it will be merely gas. But the tenth time it actually may be something quite wonderful.

Other gardeners doubtless have ideas that will make them wealthy, solve some ethereal problem or other to do with a leaky toilet, or otherwise be of some general use to themselves. In my own case, however, I can think of only one useful achievement from such thoughts—and even it is highly questionable. From time to time, as I weed, thoughts or observations pop to mind that prove useful in my writing. This chapter, for example, actually came to mind as I was weeding the rupturewort. This is an exception, however, and it does not happen often that the idea for an essay springs directly from a job at hand.

If I am excavating a particularly difficult hole, let us say, in which to plant a new buddleia, an idea may pop to mind about digging out the vegetable beds that I had undertaken some months before. Then, perhaps six months later when I'm neck-deep in trimming the multi- flora rose, I will have a sudden inspiration about excavating that particu- larly difficult hole for the buddleia. This delayed effect allows the time necessary to calm down and see the humor in what was just an ordinary, nearly tragic situation. It is very difficult, I've found to write humorously about such things as roses when I am standing neck-deep in them. Very difficult, indeed.

It is at the point of maximum inspiration—the brief apogee of mind-soar—that muscle-sore usually sets in. Muscle-sore, fatigue, thirst, and hunger, to be absolutely precise. One has been working up a dither physically and the mind has been stewing in its over-fired

synapses for quite some time. The sudden but brilliant flash of insight has temporarily blinded the gardener and he must rest. (At least that is what I tell anyone who has been unkind enough to ask why I have stopped after only ten minutes of weeding.)

We must rest, I find, to inspect our progress. To make certain that our subliminal quality-control is functioning properly. Rest to unbind the knots from underworked sinews. To refresh oneself, perhaps, from a cool tumbler of gin and tonic (or yak's milk if you prefer). To summarize our thoughts and extract from them some bit of meaning. To reflect upon any particularly profound and brilliant observation which might have arisen (often by mistake). To gather strength for yet another assault upon the garden. And finally to rise up, stumble back to the rupturewort, and ask ourselves perhaps the most significant question of human existence—"Why are there so damn many weeds?"

11
One-Legged Crickets

Why we should be forced to live in the midst of bowling greens is quite beyond my understanding. But history has decreed that we, the humble tillers of the soil, should adopt the ways of courtly England, should be ruled by majesty's sensibilities, and should be forever enslaved to the care of green spikes poking skyward from the ground.

That is the theory at least—I mean the part about "green spikes"—but if one were to peer closely at the typical American lawn, they might be a bit surprised at what was actually poking what. And as my lawn is as typical as 99% of American lawns, the reader need only substitute a few regional plant names for those I shall use and the overall effect will be about the same—we will both be cataloging "the great American tragedy."

Let us start with the grasses themselves, probably the least abundant species of any plant in the lawn and therefore quickly disposed of. The grasses in my lawn, when I can find any that is, seem to consist of three types. There are the tufts of crabgrass which erupt between infrequent mowings into mushroom clouds of despair. There are the battalions of Bermuda grass which go creeping off across every unprotected border they can locate. And occasionally I even find a few blades of what might be Kentucky bluegrass, but they really pose no threat so I don't let them worry me much.

After the grasses come what I call the good-weeds, the ones I don't have the heart to pull. In fact I mow around them when they bloom because they are generally more picturesque than the nearby garden flowers. For example, there are a few patches of ajuga which throw their purple bloom upwards in the spring. They are so alive with bumble bees that even if I didn't want them (which I most definitely do) I could not find the courage to risk my life even in a running pass with the lawn mower. Likewise, a patch or two of creeping buttercup thrive and bloom in brilliant yellow clouds. Where these flowering plants came from I do not know, but they are well worth the restraint needed not to cut them each year.

The most ubiquitous of the good-weeds is a species of violet that has spread throughout the entire lawn and shall be there long after all of us are gone. They get in everything else too, but I suppose that is a small enough price to pay for their lovely violet shades dappled throughout the garden.

Another good-weed is not a flowering plant at all but moss. This plant is indicative of shade, excessive moisture, and acidity and is listed as a lawn problem right along with "slime mold," "green scum," and "dog urine" in one popular gardening book I use. I do not consider moss a problem at all, and during the dog-days of summer, I enjoy lying on the spongy stuff and pulling out the grass seedlings which have thoughtlessly sprung up in it. I have several square yards of moss-lawn now, beneath the dense shade of a Japanese maple and some native rhododendrons. Each year I encourage its spread, paying no heed whatsoever to what the lawn book might say.

The next lawn "weed" is in a class by itself—a real beauty if one is truly objective—and the only one about which I have mixed feelings. It is the lowly, lovely dandelion. Blooming with the violets as is its wont, it is a glorious sight in the spring lawn. Possibly through ingrained social pressure I do rogue these out of the garden and remove the woody old plants from some of the lawn. I usually do this after they bloom (and usually after they've gone to seed), and I do not really object to them (as I should), but something tells me they might take over entirely if I am not somewhat careful.

I think people possess totally irrational attitudes towards the dandelion and ones which we should all try to overcome—perhaps through therapy. I say this because I am convinced that if the dandelion were not so obviously weed-like it would be greatly admired. Once, a few years removed, I planted some bulbs of *Tulipa urumiensis*, a dwarf,

multiflowered tulip with relatively splayed yellow flowers. I planted them, for want of better location, near the edge of the lawn beneath a hedge of *Ilex crenata compacta*. Surveying my garden the following spring, I saw the annual violet-dandelion show and scarcely even knew that the tulips were blooming just a bit beyond in the background. Not until I was directly upon them did I realize they probably had been blooming for several days. From a distance they were no different than a dandelion. How pretentious we gardeners are, that we do not distinguish between weed and garden except in name alone.

To emphasize this latter point I need merely give the reverse case in which coveted (by some) horticultural subjects turn upon us and become insidious pests. The worst in my lawn is ground ivy (*Glechoma hederacea*). It apparently had run rampant for years before I took over the place and although I have bested this beast in the beds, I cannot loosen it from the lawn. I have, unbelievably, seen its use touted in gardening books, but to my mind it is worse than the maligned dandelion. Why, then, do we not see the dandelion suggested for our flower beds?

Another example of equally misguided mindsets is the mock (or Indian) strawberry (*Duchesnea indica*) which at least is an attractive little groundcover but spreads wantonly from the lawn to everywhere it will. It is most interesting that in the aforementioned lawn book, mock strawberry is listed as a good groundcover (not a weed as in my lawn and flower beds), whilst the creeping buttercup (a welcome and attractive grower in my lawn) is considered a weed. Interesting, isn't it, how easily we confuse ourselves?

Having buffeted our way through the paltry few blades of grass and other more or less two-faced inhabitants of our lawn, I think we must now admit to what is left, namely all the other plants commonly known as weeds. And these most probably really are weeds (and thus sinister)—but who quite knows anymore? Included are such bounders as wild garlic (or onion), chickweed, wire grass, nut grass, plantain, red sorrel, yellow ground sorrel, and clover (at least in my "lawn"). There undoubtedly are more species than herein listed, but they are not common enough to mention. (One area of lawn near the moss beds, for example, is composed of shaved *Rhododendron maximum* seedlings, but I do not wish to precipitate a battle over whether or not these actually are weeds.)

If we take all of these plants together, then, the weedy grasses and the other good-, bad-, and ambivalent weeds, we have an approximation of what I call my lawn. At least it is green 30% of the time) and is mown (half as often as it should be). It is also disappearing as rapidly as I can replace it with other things.

In the six years I have known it, my lawn has not been fertilized, intentionally watered, dethatched, limed, aerated, reseeded, or drenched in chemicals (either for insects or diseases, and obviously not for weeds or I would have no lawn). Yet I was pleasantly surprised last spring when someone asked me how I managed to create such a lush green lawn? (Something was obviously lush, but I doubt it had much to do with lawns.) I could only reply that the results derived from doing nearly nothing—and that seemed like quite enough to me.

Lest you accuse me of doting on this accomplishment I reply that mine is not a great lawn . . . not even a good lawn. It is just a green lawn that survives the best it can and not much more. Not much different, in fact, than most other lawns I have seen. And probably like many of my fellow lawn owners, I even begrudge what little work I do put into it.

Actually it is not too clear to me why people fuss so much about lawns. Everyone, it seems, wants one, but no one really wants to take care of it. Interestingly, however, it also seems as if everyone raises an eyebrow if the neighbor does not take care of his. I would feel terribly self-conscious living in a neighborhood with houses surrounded by huge lawns which everyone else could see. If I could afford such a place I probably would be kicked out of the neighborhood for vagrancy.

In many respects I resent the lawn and all of its required lawn-think philosophy. In America, at least, we have replaced a rich and diverse prairie of meadow flora (and fauna) with a monotonous, sterile expanse of weedy-sod and a smelly, noise-ridden power mower. There are a few courageous individuals, and I am not one, who have tried to buck this age-old lawn trend by saying: "Look here, I want my lawn to be a wildflower meadow as it once was meant to be. No more cutting, no more edging, no more fertilizers, lime, dethatching, or pesticides. No! I want to grow a wildflower meadow of native plants and grasses. I want the bees and the butterflies to return; I want to see the birds increase; I want to see and smell all of summer's natural order." What they see instead, these suburban renegades, is a court order to mow the "trash heap" they call a meadow.

Suddenly it seems as if a semi-naturalized plot of earth has become the city dump. Never mind the unresurrected car set up on blocks (i.e., sans wheels) in the driveway down the road—it is of no concern. Or the white-painted tires overflowing with dead petunias and marigolds that wished they were. Pay no heed to the blue-capped gnome peering into the seahorse birdbath. Or the scalped earth spotted ever-brown with dead tufts of grass—after all it is called a lawn and it is cut (to the quick), and a rose by any other name is still a rose (sort of). Note the naked wire fence with rusty post caps, the wooden fence tumbling over its climbing rose, the brick driveway posts brutalized by a quarter-century of chromium. These are perfectly acceptable to the

majestrates of decorum. But let a few black-eyed Susans or yarrow poke above the sod and we are off to jail with a vengeance. Let some erigeron erupt, some poppies pop, some blazing-stars blaze and we're dragged off in the middle of the night to suffer the Sod Society's Inquisition.

Actually the poor devil of a suburban naturalist who wishes to return to nature (i.e., who wishes not to waste his time cutting the lawn) is increasingly hounded by commerce to do just that. At every turn now we see commercially prepared "Meadows-in-a-Bucket" or "Sods-in-a-Sack" designed to bring us back 'round to nature.' And these we find not in some sleazy, X-rated garden center, but rather in the catalogs of the more prestigious yuppy-ware emporiums. "Meadows by Manet" is not yet another French impressionist subdivision, but rather a "lawn by number" product which allows us to create masterpieces of fuzzy-naturalistic art where once our front lawn grew.

Wildflowers are now commercially in, but legally out . . . if such is possible in a society where money not only talks but demands large lecturer fees to do so. Fear not, however, a solution appears to be close at hand . . . crafted perhaps by an unnatural coalition of bottled-meadow manufacturers and politicians with old cars on blocks. The solution is perfectly simple it would seem—it is acceptable to have a meadow for a lawn if it looks like a flower bed and not a four-month vacation from mowing. If one must have a meadow, we are told by knowing exponents of the law, then one must surround the meadow with a mown strip of "lawn." This compromise indicates to all of our neighbors, you see, that yes, we do have a lawn which we cut regularly, but the patch in the middle that you might call a bed of weeds is actually what I call a meadow. Everyone is now happy. Presumably. At least legally.

These finely split semantics between your lawn and my weed-patch are all grave problems to be certain. And times, as we are all aware, are grave indeed—it seems to come with the turf. We are prepared to scalp and monotonize the land with introduced plants, yet we rebel at returning our borrowed plots of land to their rightful plants.

But perhaps we have not yet even begun to explore the really grave issues of our time. The plants are one thing, but our trespass on the prairie might perhaps be overshadowed by even more sinister thoughts on original sod. Dare we concentrate more fully on the purely physical impact of the mowing process itself?

Have you ever looked at a lawn—I mean really looked? There is an entire cosmos of life there and we humans, as is our way, feel no remorse at all when we lop it into fragments on a weekly (three-weekly in my case) basis.

Take crickets, for instance. My lawn, towards high summer, begins to look like a cricket farm. One cannot move through the grass without herding dozens of black jumping-jacks forward at every step. They drive the cats to absolute distraction.

Each cricket starts out his or her life with six legs, yet by summer's end a quick count will show a high percentage of one-legged crickets. Where do you suppose all those legs have gone? Need I explain in livid detail? The mind reels at the absolute carnage which has taken place. Fortunately for us we cannot hear the crickets scream because the lawn mower is making too much noise. But if we could, would we stop? I wonder.

Crickets are not the only victims, of course, in fact they are probably relatively well-off when the death- (and missing parts-) knell is heard. To their ranks must be added the honeybee which innocently sips at a violet, or bumblebee cruising the ground ivy. A few moths spring up from time to time, fleeing the mower's advance, while a few thousand chinch bugs and leafhoppers presumably are ground-up as the year grinds on. During the lawn murdering season, who can guess how many ants are crushed under the rolling wheels of fate; how many tens of thousands of mites, curiously wandering about the grass blades, are suddenly sucked into the whirring blades of mastication? I don't really want to know. I think the responsibility would weigh too heavily upon my shoulders.

Insects, however, are expendable as everyone knows. The fewer the better. Most people swat a fly with no remorse at all. But a fly is an individual life form just as is a tiger or a panda, or even an elephant. We, however, being supreme in all things, judge the fly as not worthy of life. If an elephant were the same size as a fly we would dispose of it just as readily. Humans seem to be peculiar that way.

On towards midsummer my lawn becomes infested with another life form which is just slightly harder for humans to do-in— perhaps because these forms produce slightly less hostility than insects. These are the tiny toadlets that have just emerged from my once tadpole-infested pond. They emerge by the hundreds to be ground underfoot on the terrace, to be the unwilling objects of cat brutality, and to suffer the cutting edge of the lawn mower. I cannot mow the lawn when this eruption occurs; in fact it is all I can do to garden. The toads are in nearly every trowelful of earth and every bunch of weeds pulled. I would become a living wart if I were to garden at this time of year, so I don't (see future chapters for other labor-saving excuses).

One step up from little toads is big toads and frogs. Mercifully I have encountered few of these in my mowings. And they are so big, in fact, that they may easily be seen fleeing well in advance of the blades of doom; thus one theoretically has the opportunity to avoid them (and a few of the psychopathic wretches amongst us probably would take the opportunity not to). Still in all, as careful a mower as I am, I can still remember vividly the twitching hindleg of a leopard frog as it flopped about helplessly on the front sidewalk after a pass-by with the mower. I did not find the hapless owner of the leg, but its ghost still haunts me as I push on with my whirring instrument of death.

Of those creatures without legs—and thus statistically less likely victims to lose a limb—I have little to say. On several occasions I have startled snakes from my lawn, but they are inspiredly swift and rather low down so I never worry about them—at least not enough to mention. To my knowledge I've never decapitated a slug, but then nobody's perfect. I hope fervently that I've mashed a few under the wheels, but actually I have no slime-counts by which to reckon this factor. Similarly I've never as much as seen half a worm, so I can happily suppose that they remain unscathed in my efforts at tonsorial beauty.

But having briefly tallied the truly sad fate of the lesser beasties of the field, I find that perhaps I have not yet finished the horrible tales of rotary mayhem. You need not worry at this point, however, that I will go into gruesomely true stories of my hunting expeditions for larger game such as mice, squirrels, dogs, bunny rabbits, or my neighbors' children. Of these larger beasts I can safely say that hunting with a lawn mower is quite fair game, so to speak; I've never hit anything larger than a frog and I'd just as soon keep it that way.

No, my mind is not on the larger animals or even on animals at all. Instead I am thinking of that most malevolent of all crimes . . . horticide. For there is a body of humankind who insist that plants have feelings just as humans do. These are such delicate creatures—the humans, that is—that even to pluck a fruit from amongst the apple tree's limbs would cause instant grief. So attuned to nature's lifeline are they that no hostility may be demonstrated to any plant; even fruit may not be eaten until it presumably dies of old age—that is, it falls off the mother-plant of its own accord.

I trust these people do not have lawns, or lawn mowers, for the agonizing chorus of thousands upon thousands of tiny, decapitated grassblades might be emotionally too demanding. Ajuga would royally herald the coming of the blades with great paeans until one by one their bugles fell silent. Shrieking violets—Antoinette-like losing their dainty heads—would proclaim "let them eat cake" in multiplicious voices as the mower ran down the row of beauties. And alternatively the dandelions would roar their kingly disapproval of the entire affair, at once a most disquieting situation, but historically natural for the royal family.

I am not altogether certain that plants have feelings—I would rather think they don't. So it bothers me very little that a few people will dine tonight on well-rotted broccoli rather than shed its sap by physical violence. It would be best, perhaps, not to mention the millions of living bacteria that they will boil to death while preparing such spiritually gained fruits, or that they might choke upon while eating righteously fallen apples. So I won't. But I do protest the creation of one-legged crickets and ask for the crickets' sake that you return your sod to nature's keeping, or failing that, at least put a horn on your lawnmower.

12
Pause for Paws

I suppose as I have already broached the subject of animals in the garden I may as well continue on with the subject and get it over with all at once. It may as well be admitted that a garden is only a small part of the rest of the world . . . a sort of "detached reality" as it were . . . and so we must deal with all of the bits and pieces of gardening, be they vegetable, mineral, or animal. It is the animal bits that are tugging at me this very moment, and I fear they will not rest until ceded to.

On the table, as I write (try to, is perhaps a better description), is a fearsome black and white animal who is elegantly chewing at something or other between his toes. Between paw-gnaws he growls portentously at his younger housemate who is ascending my leg as if it were a trail by which the table top might be reached. Both of these creatures smell awfully much like spoiled mackerel and rightly so, as they have just finished their usual late-night snack. It is now my duty to scratch various parts of their anatomy before they take their baths and retire for the evening.

Sometimes they check up on my progress with this book, just to see how it's going and to see if I've reached the part about them. (Whoops, Cleo just sat on my writing pad so I'll have to stop for a moment and push her to the far side of the table. Now that's over with I can continue.) As I was saying, sometimes they check on my progress. Bruno, that's the older fellow, has gone so far tonight as to take the pen in his mouth and write some "cat." Unfortunately, or perhaps fortunately, it is none too legible. He now asks me, in his inimitable chirping fashion, to tell you of his exciting adventure this evening. He is quite insistent that I do this (one paw is on the pad and he grips the pen in his teeth) but I shall only pretend to write if that is acceptable to you. (He does tend to go on so.) Actually the gist of the story is that he just caught this mouse out back in the field and gave it to his friend Cleo— between the two of us, that is about all he is able to give his female acquaintances. But then this other, very big black cat from across the way (who possibly has a great deal more to offer) came over and took it for himself. Bruno did his best to stare down the bully, he assures me, but the story does not end well . . . especially for the mouse. There's really not all that much to the story except, perhaps, that cats are not terribly much unlike people. So I will end it. Bruno thinks I am going to go on at length about this happening, but we shall know differently. It is always best to let him think he is having his way because he will now leave me alone long enough so I can write something possibly worthwhile. (Meanwhile Cleo has just knocked over an ice bucket and the invaluable plans for the new sewer so I will have to get back to you in a moment.)

Well, that's taken care of, but now Bruno has returned to see if I put in the part about his "staring down the bully" . . . this as he squats in front of my light and licks his . . . well his . . . his you know what. Now Cleo has joined the fun and is all over the paper, and I really must stop for the night, I am only human you know.

Well that's better now. Another night and all is well. The cats are off on a tear downstairs totally unmindful of my diligence yet again at the blank pad. Let us hope it stays that way.

Much has been written about cats and undoubtedly more shall be written, for cats take well to paper—so to speak. Much better than dogs, actually, but that is quite another story, indeed. I don't care much for dogs, but then why should I? I've only been badly bitten on a few occasions, but then that really has little to do with the problem. Neither does the constant jumping nor yapping seem to bother me much. Drooling and slobbering, on the other hand (or foot, or wherever), certainly do begin to get to the heart of things so to speak. As does the irritating habit of public crotch sniffing.

It is rather awkward, I find, to stand in someone's hallway . . . perhaps a stranger or even a good acquaintance . . . trying to balance polite conversation against the cautious (and hopefully unobserved) movements as one's hand pushes some strange dog's nose out of one's private parts. (The dog's owner, although looking at one's hands, evidently never ascertains the real significance of the problem and seems to think that one is entertaining the dog. Owners . . . much like their dogs . . . are not very bright in these matters.)

Cats and (unwanted) dogs are a part of my garden, as they are a part of almost everyone's. In my case I favor cats and stone the dogs (though I am a terribly poor marksman). But these are by no means the only denizens of my garden "zoo." As I mentioned in the previous chapter, my garden has its quota of bugs (both bad and good . . . my neighbor, for example, has four hives of bees but I have all the nectar) and of frogs, worms, toads, snakes, and myriads of unseen microscopic lifeforms. These are part of the gardner, and my philosophy is generally to live and let live. I scarcely use any chemicals at all, and about the only thing I try to combat (and not too well at that) is the animated slime known as slugs. They are hopeless, but as they are also hopelessly prolific I do my best to plan their parenting with a liberal dose of slugicide.

All of these creatures are what might be termed the lesser animals. A rather poor term, indeed, because taken in quantities of numbers they are quite endlessly numerous. And taken in terms of weight of living tissue (technically called biomass) they probably outweigh me ten to one. But lesser animals they are, simply because they are too small or cryptic to see and because they are not terribly attractive to us when we do see them.

On the other hand, furry creatures with cute-little-sparkley-eyes or big-dopey-looking ones, are acceptable to us as worthy of the name "real" animal. These are the animals that television shows and books are made of. I've had several such animals living in my garden, but I must say I would prefer they stick to their television roles.

Take the woodchuck, for instance. As big as any cocker spaniel and as burrowy as any worm, this woodchuck lived in the walk-in storage space under my screenporch. He (or she . . . we were never formally introduced) tunneled down outside the brick wall that supports the porch, under the concrete foundation, and eventually came up through the earthen floor of the storage area. As I was later to discover there was a great mound of earth heaped up on the outside wall, but this was obscured by five or six azaleas (they probably would have died in a few months from want of air). Inside, a number of objects had quietly been buried while I paid absolutely no attention . . . the bathtub to name one.

Not that I normally bathe in the store room, mind you, I was merely storing an old claw-foot tub for a friend of mine who left no forwarding address. The tub was half full of red clay tailings when I finally noticed something was not quite right. Next to this the oil tank was partially covered, as was a small collection of antique bricks I had acquired for some odd reason or other. Also a number of clay pots were now beneath ground level and an entire box of plastic pots lay protruding as if from some red lava flow.

We existed, this woodchuck and I, for some months that I know about and possibly many more that I didn't. I never saw any evidence of plant damage nor, in fact, did I even see much evidence of the woodchuck; only the tunnel and on one occasion a fat ball of fur sitting on its haunches in my driveway. This immediately dashed to the tunnel upon seeing me (I have this curious effect on some people as well). Within a few months of discovery, however, I unintentionally made life for the poor creature rather unbearable.

As my porch was in a terminal state of decay (two or three human feet had already gone through the floorboards), and I needed some extra living space myself, the whole structure was demolished and carted away. This, by itself, probably had little effect on the tunneler, but when they brought in the bulldozer to excavate 6 feet of soil for a new basement, I think the woodchuck felt that it had met its tunneling match. Our paths have not crossed since.

Another real animal that I inadvertently evicted from a home was the opossum. I use "I" in the imperial sense as I only caused it to be ousted. It was actually the treeman who did the foul deed . . . and extremely reluctantly, too, I might add. He had other plans on his mind than simple eviction. The treeman was halfway up a rotten old willow— if rot and decay seem to you a rampant problem in my environment you are a very perceptive reader—when he came face to face (or perhaps face to vice versa) with a possum in a big ball of twigs and leaves. The treeman backed off rapidly, shouting down in somewhat guarded hysteria that possums had "real sharp teeth and lots of them" and he didn't reckon on "arguing with no possum twenty feet up in no tree." (I have edited and paraphrased the exact quote as there were some words I don't believe I heard quite right.)

At first the treeman was simply going to cut off half the tree and let the possum fall where it might. But with a little persuasion a gallery of us onlookers talked him into lowering the limb in question with some pullies and ropes. He went along with the idea, but an astute observer might have questioned his enthusiasm. When finally the possum hit ground it ambled nonchalantly off as if this sort of thing happened rather more frequently than one had imagined.

The woodchuck and the possum have been the two largest furry creatures to grace my garden (dogs notwithstanding). And while I've seen others of their kind in my neighborhood, I've never seen them on my own property. I've never seen a raccoon here either, but they must certainly be around, as are the deer, for I've seen them down the road a bit.

Of small furry creatures I have my share. The cats of course are an integral part of the garden; my own cats, as well as several others who drop by from time to time to salvage breakfast from Bruno's bowl as he looks on. In addition there are also the chipmunks, the bats, the squirrels, the rabbits, and the moles, the latter three of which could all be shot as far as I care.

The squirrels are constantly rearranging plants, usually for the worse, but, more seriously, they are always gathering walnuts from my neighbor's yard and burying them in mine. I don't like walnuts, especially when they come up in the rock garden. Squirrels have scarcely any sense of proportion.

The rabbits have the nasty habit of eating all the flower buds off my young azaleas. And if I grew vegetables they'd eat those as well (I have this on record from my knowledgeable vegetable-growing friends). On several occasions one or other of my cats have brought rabbits into the house—alive or dead, it doesn't seem to matter to them . . . the cats, that is. It is always a pleasant surprise to find some bloody mess or other in front of the television.

The most devastating of the small furries would have to be the moles. And I *do* have a bumper crop of moles from time to time. They dislodge all sorts of small plants from the soil, but more aggravating are the runs they dig which may occur anywhere. In the rockery they dislodge and bury small stones with no sign of compassion at all, and in the perennial beds they make the ground look . . . look . . . well, I guess you'd have to say wrinkled. They are particularly bad on the terrace, though, as they tunnel between the flagstone paving, pushing sand and gravel up all over the surface. This is particularly annoying if one wants things to look nice, because the effect is not exactly picture-book pleasing.

I have tried to control these moles by various means, none of which come close to working. Flooding with a garden hose seems to lead nowhere and only makes everything muddy. Traps with sinister looking springs and daggers going off in every direction are particularly ineffective. Poisoned peanuts seem not to work at all . . . especially on the children next door. And gas bombs don't seem to affect anything except me. Nothing is effective against moles. Not even cats. And that is saying something. Not much, but something.

Another animal against which cats are totally ineffective is mice. Not field mice, mind you, they do somewhat of a job on those (after all cats do have a reputation to uphold). No, it is the house mice I'm thinking of . . . particularly the varieties called aquatic mice, floor mice, and sunflower mice. These are rare varieties (not the least bit endangered except the first) found only in the vicinity of my house.

Aquatic mice are the least of my worries . . . at least since I emptied the aquarium. I'd never heard of them myself, until shortly after I'd moved into the house and was throwing an afternoon dinner party. The previous residents had built some small aquariums into the wall of the basement, one of which had been used for fish and the other two as terrariums. Upon moving they had taken all of the fish from the aquarium but thoughtfully had left the water. (The plants in the terrariums were in various stages and extremes of death, but I really need not mention this as they are irrelevant for the rest of the story.)

During the course of events, one of the female guests came up to me and said that I really should come and take a look at my aquarium. I thought this an odd suggestion at first, but then realized that I had been away from the social graces for years and that Washington functions were quite unlike any I was used to. I thought, perhaps, that aquariums had replaced etchings in the more trendy circles. I scarcely expected to find a dead aquatic mouse floating in the half-filled tank. Actually I thought they were better swimmers than that. Several weeks later I found another, and that was when I emptied the tank. Since then I have seen no more aquatic mice . . . not even in the pond.

The sunflower mouse is another variety that occurs in my house. I have never actually seen this one in action . . . just the results of its industriousness. One afternoon when I was cleaning rather more carefully than usual—a once a year project—I decided to take the cushions off the sofa and collect any loose change that might have fallen in the crevices. Instead, under the first cushion I found a pile of sunflower seeds neatly tucked away in the corner. At least half a cup by any sort of reckoning. This I picked up somewhat bewilderedly, unable to recall the last time I had hidden sunflower seeds for any reason. (I knew Bruno had not done it because he uses sunflower seeds only for bait when he goes birding.) Friends were out of the question as I either did not have any at the time or, if I did, none that I knew of were likely to be seed horders.

I moved on to the middle of the three cushions and found nothing there, but another pile of seeds appeared at the end of the sofa under the third cushion. And yet another pile under the love seat cushions. Three piles of sunflower seeds under three cushions . . . but from where? And how? Perhaps I lived in a house of parapsychological phenomena. I'd heard of bent forks (even had a few in the drawer) and mysterious writings (those were in the drawer, too), but never sunflower seed apparitions. Did I need a seed-buster? Not as it turned out.

One day, while cleaning the basement—a once a decade project—I ran across a bag of sunflower seeds. An old bag I'd had at least two years. Twenty-five pounds worth (it had been a Christmas present to Bruno). Suddenly I knew where the seeds had come from (I don't have a PhD for nothing, it turns out). How they had moved upstairs and into my sofa is just a guess, but I think it was sunflower mice. The bottom of the bag had been gnawed into and sunflower seeds were strewn everywhere around the base. The aquatic mice had climbed three-quarters of the way up the wall for a swim so it was no great task for a seed-hiding mouse to go the extra two feet to the first floor. (I'm almost positive they came up behind the stove because I saw a mouse there once . . . but I thought it was a stove mouse.) Whatever method they used, the number of seeds sequestered away would have required dozens of trips. There are hundreds of places to store seeds in the basement . . . most of them disturbed only every ten years or so. Why mice should make such a great trip to the sofa is beyond me. I figure sunflower mice just have more class than your average mouse.

And then there there were the noises of the night. A tail of intrigue and deduction and a worthless cat.

For some few days after first moving into my house, I would wake up at three in the morning—mind half gone—to the sounds of scrapings and tappings coming from the ceiling. In the beginning I presumed it was the house talking as it frequently does—the endless creaking and moaning conversations that houses have with themselves. For weeks I lived with the situation. Every morning at two or three a.m., there were the noises. It was too regular, I finally realized one groggy morning, to be a talking house. I decided it was bats. Bats that returned from hunting every night, flew into the attic through the vent, and finally snuggled into the wall cavity just above my head.

After a while the noises either stopped or I got used to them. All was quiet for several years until suddenly, one morning at three a.m., the sounds returned. This time they arrived at a time when I was not in the mood for routine morning awakenings. After a few evenings I decided something had to be done and I was the one who would have to do it.

One morning, as sounds were being generated, I stood up from the nice warm bed into the freezing darkness and followed them to an apparent source in the ceiling. The next day I measured off the distance from the side wall and went upstairs to see what might be seen. The sound emanated from the upstairs closet floor . . . a fairly unlikely place for bats I finally conceded. However, the floor was fairly unlikely in itself, as it was not so much a floor as a convoluted wooden structure built over a hot air duct. Several minutes with a crowbar and hammer uncovered a mass of insulation, ductwork, floor joists, and a half-full can of lighter fluid (no, don't even bother to ask . . . I don't have any ideas either!).

Because of the maze-like atmosphere of the space I began to smell a rat . . . well, actually a mouse was more like it. So for several nights I forced Bruno to sleep upstairs and to do his fair share of the work around the place (he is generally as worthless as any child could be in this respect).

A week later the noises were still waking me up. So I went out and bought a mousetrap. The next morning I had a mouse and that was that.

I'm not too awfully keen on animals living in the house with me (sometimes not even cats), but I do enjoy, to some extent or other, the fact that my garden provides a place of sanctuary to many of nature's creatures. Planting a garden is one of the small ways in which we humans can repay the animals for occupying land that really belongs to them. That is why I cannot become overly distressed when, for example, the moles do their worst to undermine my hard-labored work. I resign myself to accept nature's way as best I can. Who am I to quarrel with the rightful owners?

On the other hand, whenever Bruno gets to behaving unduly uppity I show no mercy. I go straight to the drawer, get the mousetrap, and stick it in his face just to remind him that we all have to pull together around here. After all, at least one of us could easily be replaced by something that actually works.

101

13
Summer Thoughts
(and some are opinions)

As a rule gardeners (or perhaps more likely garden writers) seem not to care much for summer, especially high summer. Paeans are raised to spring's awakening, fall is celebrated for its harvests of color, and some even extol winter's virtue of quiet beauty and garden challenge. At best high summer is referred to as a "bridge," as if we must hurry to cross over from July to October before something dreadful happens. Henry Mitchell (*The Essential Earthman*) perhaps sums up the matter when he admonishes that "the average garden goes to pot on July 16 as regular as clockwork."

I make no pretense myself. Summer is the season for me. Spring is much to iffy, too tentative. It can't decide if it wants to desert winter's cold ways or embrace summer's warmth. So it fidgets back and forth aiming for compromise and pleasing all but me. Fall is far too portending. It knows what is about to happen so it pulls in all its reserves, leaving everything naked to fend for itself against what must soon follow. And winter is, is . . . well . . . is simply too awful for words.

Summer, however, is plainly straightforward: summer is summer, as we know, and that is that. You cannot say the same for winter, which on any given day may be winter, spring, summer, or fall. Within the past three weeks, for example, beginning with December 29th, my garden has had temperatures ranging from 78°F to −8°F. There is something terribly wicked about a season that messes about like that. You don't see differences of 86° in the days of July, August, or even September, now, do you? No. Summer is summer and that is that.

In my climate, at least, gardeners must keep themselves shuttered away from winter's rages for nearly three months. This means that the storm windows go up, the furnace goes on, and the gardener goes into shock. Not so in summer. At least not me. The windows are thrown open, the furnace is shut down, and the gardener goes to work.

Many argue that we need air conditioning in our climate, but I say they ought to move to Florida if they want air conditioning. I have central air but I don't use it. I rely instead on open windows and doors, a cool basement on excruciatingly bad days, a dash of dehumidifier, and controlled lethargy for good measure. I cannot—nay, will not—close myself inside the house all summer as I am forced to do in winter. It is inhumane to one's self to be perpetually locked up as if one were some sort of criminal.

The windows must be opened to let summer's mellowed breezes permeate the house; to chase out every last vestige of winter's spite in places which even spring could not reach. We must listen as summer's orchestra begins to fine tune: the crickets and katydids as they rasp newfound wings (and urges) into public romance; the frogs and toads with pneumatic organs bellowing for attention; the cicadas with their high-pitched, tympanic outbursts. These sounds assure us, day or night, that life is in its utmost season and hadn't we ought to listen-up? Pity those poor souls who listen instead to the deadly sounds of whirring motors and grinding fans—those who muffle reality.

(The one really perverse side to summer's sound is that of the power-mower squadrons whose attacks may come at almost any time of day or night. I take great satisfaction in the fact that as natural sounds increase with summer's heat, those of the grim reapers grow ever dimmer as each day slowly burns the grass to brown.)

With summer's emergence comes an air of languid exuberance—a feel of sullen lushness which hangs heavily upon our garden and body as we work. We rejoice in the primeval warmth and fluidity from whence we arose eons ago. Perhaps we recall some sense of the original garden and its eagerly robust liveliness. Perhaps it is a long-buried sense of lust which is suddenly released from remote holds of time. We feel as one with the soil and the growth it produces. There is no other time in the garden like this.

Starting eagerly in the morning, with no thought of outer wear, no fear of cold, we calculate what needs to be done, rough out the day's time-schedule, then head off to our destinies.

This day I must weed the lower path near the shed (yes, again, I tell myself—the third time since June); the rock wall near the pond needs another 2–3 feet of progress; I've got to move a pile of something (the nature of the pile is irrelevant, moving piles is a standard, year-round duty—what you might call a generic task); I'll mow the lawn if I have a chance (damn); and I suppose I'd best water too.

And so off I go, first turning on the water, then getting the bucket and burlap for the weeding job. In a few hours that is finished and I'm off to the rock wall, but first I think, perhaps I'll have lunch. I haven't eaten since the last time, and this seems like a good breaking point. An hour later I'm back to the rock pile.

This is a very creative thing this rock wall stuff and it requires much consideration. I work slowly at first, taking deliberate measure of each rock. As I progress the work becomes increasingly slower until I reach a point in the mid-day's sun when I must stop altogether and reconsider things just a bit. To help I concoct a wine-cooler, then find a shady spot under the Japanese maple.

Here I study the quality of my rock work and determine the next turn of direction; my mind starts to cloud slightly—to drift. The heat has begun to take its toll, aided no doubt by a certain amount of labor and perhaps a little wine. I look at the garden in full light and it takes on a disquieting reserve, as if it might not stand the scrutiny of too few shadows. The shabbiness is illuminated a little more than seems polite,

105

and I realize the imperfections perhaps more than I should. I dote on the garden and what it should be, on what it could be and I wonder, somewhat dazedly, if all this gardening stuff is really what anyone had in mind for humankind.

Wouldn't nature, I reason somewhat in a heat haze, be better off if man didn't keep struggling so hard to rearrange it to his own specifications? Gardeners are particularly bad at this, actually, as we are continually introducing every foreign and exotic plant (whether natural or engineered) to our little plots of the earth. Petunias from South America, zinnias and marigolds from Mexico, tulips and daffodils from Turkey, pelargoniums from Africa, chrysanthemums from China, Iceland poppies from Siberia. The list would be endless if we could untangle the geographical histories of our commonest garden plants; it would be hopeless if we could untangle the genetics of our hybrids and their natural parents.

Actually I'm not really too worried about gardeners and their antics. They probably contribute relatively little to the rearrangement of floras, they increase the diversity of green things within their earthly plots, and they may even help to conserve native plants from abuse at the hands of normal humankind. In reality, however, there are so few gardeners, at least in this country, that I doubt they have much effect on anything except to keep each other amused.

No, the real problem as I see it is that there are too many so-called gardens in the United States and so few gardeners. As I have only just belabored the state of the American lawn in a previous chapter, I will say no more about it. It is only indicative of the fact that the American garden needs to have a sharp going over in my opinion.

I have driven and walked many a mile as a naturalist in this country, seen both city and country, and what strikes at my very heart is how poorly we treat our land and ourselves. I don't know why the American ethic decrees that we shall all strive to live in individual houses with a front lawn, a back yard, and arbovitae at each corner of the house—that each should own a castle.

Everyone, it seems, *wants* a house and yard, but I wonder why? Most houses come with "yards" not gardens. Yards are made of dirt and plants, sort of, and that is the extent of most of American "gardening." Somehow the gardener is eliminated from all of this and the owner becomes merely a caretaker. The majority of homeowners, in my opinion, really resent having to waste their time in the yard and as a result the average "castle" consists of little more than a mowed field and whatever else survives.

It is possibly unkind to be so blunt, but I think the great American dream ought to be revised just a bit for the benefit of future generations. The average homeowner nowadays seems to have time to do nearly everything (or practically nothing, if the truth be known) except tend to his or her property. Property, we are assured, is what we should have; it is after all first-most in material thinking. Yet maintenance of such property is last-most in most anyone's mind, especially the yard, because it is plain dirt work.

Better to watch Wednesday night football or sappy soapy operas than to till the soil. Out we go to the movies, dinner, the opera, a rock concert. But tidy-up the flower beds—not today, thanks, too much else to do. Perhaps instead of sowing so many wild oats we should sow some different sorts of seed. A few more seed packets, spades, and rakes in the hands of children is what is needed, and a lot fewer expensive, mindless toys. Cucumbers and calendulas, should be our slogan, not computers!

What this country needs is a *garden ethic* with a redefinition of the word "garden." One can no more label 90% (if one is generous) of America's yards attached to America's houses as gardens anymore than we might call a thicket of hardwoods, a briar patch, or an old-field a garden.

Now, before anyone accuses me of excessive class-conscious thinking or of garden elitism I must vigorously protest my innocence. I personally do not care what sort of garden anyone else has, in fact I truly favor the undisciplined chaos of wildflower meadows and greatly admire the cottage gardens in their true sense. What I argue against is the obsession of owning a "yard" if a person has absolutely no interest in that piece of ground other than sitting on it. Better these people live in mile-high apartments and save the land for those of us who wish to garden with a passion. Everyone would be better off.

Also in defense of self, I would like to establish that I do not equate size of garden, or splendor of garden, or even richness of material ornamentation with quality of garden. A square foot can be as lovely as any botanical garden, perhaps even lovelier in its own comprehensible way.

A garden is defined not so much by the amount of its space or money spent, not even by its plants. It is defined by its conscious arrangement of plants. And its arrangement of plants is determined by its arranger, or as he or she is better known, its gardener. It is only natural to me that these two ingredients—plants and gardener—are what define a garden. You can't have one without the other.

Some might say that the Japanese "sand garden" is an example of a garden with a gardener but no plants. If the space has but one plant it is a garden; perhaps even the highest form of garden and gardening known to humankind. For the interaction of gardener, plant, and earth would ensure the spiritual unity of all three. Without that plant, however, the sand garden would be merely a sandbox and its caretaker either a devoutly rakish philosopher or an existential cat fancier. Who knows, perhaps the two are not intellectually all that far apart.

On the other hand, an exquisitely beautiful, untouched alpine meadow might be considered by some to be a garden of unmatched splendor. Even if it had ten times a million plants I could not call it a garden for it has had no one to arrange it (for better or worse—and HE does not count). If someone took six plants from the meadow and arranged them in a container (no matter how badly) then we have created a dish garden, or an alpine trough, or an alpine pot (or pan as the British say, though I don't know why—the British use so many peculiar words I often wonder if they do it just to keep us confused).

*   *   *   *

I start suddenly—from jumbles of Japanese pans, sandy alpine dishes, and British confusion—to a presence, of sorts, trodding across my stomach. I realize Bruno has rescued me from nodding off entirely in the afternoon's lull. Here I am, almost asleep, cerebrally prattling on about quality of gardens when I should be working to improve my own poor example. Unfortunately I fall easy victim to summer's lilting "slow-but-certainly" banner, but perhaps I should be permitted my mid-day siesta without too many disapproving nods.

I do not mean to imply that summer might be used as an excuse not to work (but that *is* one added attraction). No! I mean that with the days being so long and all, and the air just a bit weighty, it is appropriate to pace one's self—for the good of the body, that is. I use such occasions merely as an interlude between fits and snatches of real work; just one method to keep from overheating.

On those very few occasions when I am found sprawled inelegantly on the lawn—looking for signs of chinch bugs or inspecting the cloud formations for signs of rain—it is often difficult to explain to those who insist on idly "dropping by" that I am actually formulating my next attack on the garden and not just snoozing as they seem to suspect. One must organize and divide to conquer, and I do this best in a prone position.

But I suppose if you insist that I return to tending summer's garden I will simply have to do so. Where was I then? Oh yes, now I remember, the rock wall. I rise from the ground and walk slowly towards the wall. My, the lawn's edge is looking a bit shabby (I'll remember to trim it—next month, perhaps). Probably ought to dead-head those daylilies (drat, forgot the cutters; I'll catch up on that when I trim the lawn). Aren't the water lilies nice; I'd better count to see if I have a new record (21 blooms is the old one). Best to start thinking about staking the cone-flowers (in fact that's just what I'll do—think about it; they'll survive another month or two without it, maybe even 'til winter). Really should finish up that rock wall this afternoon, too (really better wait until the sun drops a bit—say about 30° to the south).

If it might appear to you as if I spend a lot of time resting—for a gardener, that is—it is because my summers for the past few years have been filled with various forms of semi-herculean tasks. And not much in the way of flower growing. As you may recall I built a terrace (several times) over the first few years, not to mention moving mounds of earth, rock, gravel, and sand. And moving objects as many times as I do doubtless causes me to rest perhaps more than I should.

But this will all be changing in, say, the next 15 or 20 years because I have finally reached a point where plants are actually beginning to almost nearly take as much time as sand, gravel, rocks, flagstones, manure, sod-moving, composting, hacking, pruning, lawnmowing, napping (whoops, I mean mapping), and the other essentials of gardening. I mean plants are really the last thing you need in a garden—they clutter up the place something awful.

14
Battle of the Bulbs

There arrives a time each year when summer's mantle simply grows too heavy. When earth withdraws from its kingly benefactor the sun and embraces more earnestly its knightly prince of darkness. A time, it seems, when even life itself wearies of its hotly passioned exuberance. Coolness stalks the night, summoning its dark forces: first to admonish with feeble-fingered warning, then to stab more vigorously, icy daggers slashing out the very essence of summer's glory. Fall has arrived with its kindly warning, and we prepare for the battle of the bulbs.

No one, I fear, is less prepared for this battle than I. For it is uphill, as they say, and signifies only one thing to me . . . the worst is yet to come. I suppose I am not a very well oriented gardener, but bulbs symbolize winter to me . . . not spring as they are supposed to do. Why this should be so must have something to do with a particularly bad rash I had as a child. It certainly has nothing to do with logic.

It is not as if winter were actually upon us, you understand. When bulb planting season arrives there is not the slightest hint of frost, not the tenderest plant battered black and purple by jack-frost's ice pick, and no bleak, leafless landscape. Little reason at all to rouse summer's gardener to winter's combat. Yet so conditioned am I by past experiences, that upon arrival of the season's first bulb catalog, I rush to the closet to find a sweater. That, of course, was when things were normal and bulb catalogs arrived in late summer. Now, however, with purveyors of bulbs sending out pre-season sale catalogs in March, I've still got my sweater on from last winter. In fact I've usually just been out admiring the narcissi and tulips, and the sellers are preparing me for next winter. It is not fair . . . but, of course, it is gardening.

Why must we gardeners always be preparing for the next "event" of the season when we have barely reached the one at hand? Because it is our lot in life, that is why. It is simply the price we pay. We must be perennially out of sync with reality so that the garden will be perpetually at its best. I have often wondered if a working definition of an avid gardener might be a "person who works every waking moment to make the future as beautiful as the past could have been." Gardeners are always striving for that illusive point in time called perfection, wherein every petal, every stem, every leaf, is just as it "should be." And, I am sorry to say, there are some sorts of people who have been known to take advantage of this slight flaw in our otherwise sterling character.

Foremost among the worst of these sorts of vagrants might be counted the bulb merchants whose seductive, photo-filled catalogs are so saturated with color that even the strongest among us cannot (thankfully) resist the temptation to create perfection. Never mind that each luscious study is a composition of 6 bulbs grown under glass and then posed in pots camouflaged with velvety green sphagnum moss, ferns, and well-placed logs. They still *look* gorgeous in the picture and will do so in our imaginary, next-spring garden. Ah, but it is here that the merchants may be outsmarting even themselves, for already their early catalogs are arriving dangerously close to reality. Close enough so that we are able to open our catalog and compare, point-for-point, imagination with fact: there, 6 lively, enticingly opened buds clustered in perfection—here, 3 semi-decumbent buds, 2 rain-knocked, half-opened flowers, and a half shattered blossom whose time has come (and gone); there, sturdy, upright foliage—here, leaves arranged as if some cat had just spent the night on them (which he had); there, the ground covered in lush green carpeting—and here, the ground appearing as if the same cat had spent the morning in vigorous excavation (which, I might add truthfully, he had).

Having succumbed, for the sake of argument, to the fact that we *shall have* bulbs despite reality, the next step, of course, must be to chose them. Shall it be tulips this year, or tulips and daffodils, or shall we have-at the lesser known bulbs? Or perhaps as a compromise we might just try everything. Let us say, to be abnormally atypical (i.e., restrained), that we opt first for tulips. Nothing could be more spring-like than tulips, or more confusing. Shall we start with the simple ones first? Say the early bloomers? With single or double earlies, or the early emperors? Perhaps we should add some late-season Darwins and cottage sorts. We could bridge the gap between the earlies and the laties with hybrid midseason Darwins that combine the best of the early emperors and the late Darwinness of the Darwins. Or we could select from among the parrot sorts, or the bouquets, or the Rembrandts; but then the lily-flowered types might be nice too, or perhaps the peony or orchid types. (Is anyone developing a tulip-type tulip I wonder?).

After we have circled (or X-ed) our way through the tulip section we should now write down what it is that we are going to order . . . on a piece of paper . . . not the order blank. Never, never on the order blank, for that would be certain disaster. You will find, as I always have, that when your tulip order is totaled, on average, it amounts to $436.51 . . . sometimes a little less, but usually a lot more. It really does not pay, so to speak, to go on to the daffodils (or even the lesser bulbs, for that matter) until you've solved the tulip problem. (I solved the tulip problem some time ago by not buying them, but this may not suit your taste. I merely point out life's little iniquities . . . if I could solve them I would most likely be writing essays on psychology and being paid vast sums of money for them.)

There is one possible way around the money problem (several, if you are wealthy) and that is by comparison shopping. Bulb prices vary quite a bit between catalogs, and especially between catalogs and garden centers. You may save a relatively substantial amount by comparing prices of one item across-the-board, but unfortunately it is not always possible to know if bulb size is constant. Also, rather unfortunately, items in catalogs are not uniformly lower priced within a single catalog. Prices may be lower for lily-flowered tulips in one catalog but Rembrandts may be higher than in other catalogs. In the end, I always end up by picking and choosing from amongst several catalogs and ordering a little from each. This is the coward's way, but it suits me, and I receive a lot of free catalogs the next year.

Regardless of what you decide to buy, from whom you buy it, or how much you pay, you should resign yourself to one of gardening's more difficult lessons . . . no matter how many bulbs you buy it will never seem to be enough. If you think 1 bulb will do, buy 2—1000, buy 2000—and so on. It is just a peculiar law of gardening that you only buy half as many of any plant as you really need.

With the preliminary skirmishes out of the way . . . the lesser battles, so to speak . . . we may now step to the fore with spade in hand to do physical combat with the bulbs. From the minute we have placed our first order until the bulbs are subdued under sod, we must all be in a constant state of agitated readiness . . . as I have found from painful experience.

Why is it, one might ask, that bulbs always arrive at the least opportune time? I mean gardening is struggle enough in the fall—what with all of the pre- and post-freeze cleaning, preparation, and protection—that we don't need another hurdle thrown across our narrow, weed-strewn path. Yet on the afternoon we least need them, there they sit in their just-delivered, brown-paper box, begging for attention. As soon as you touch the box, of course, it begins to rain (if we're lucky), or snow, or sleet, or some other such depravity of nature. Anything to turn the soil to mud. The rain will keep up, usually, for as long as it takes to use up the amount of time which would have been available had we but had the time to plant the damn things. This is usually until Monday morning. And then, when you're off to work, the sun comes out. It will be a balmy, Indian-summer week, the soil will dry out perfectly by Friday, and then it will rain again on Saturday morning. If, by chance, you should think about staying home on Wednesday because the weather looks so good . . . don't bother; it will rain on Wednesday *and* Saturday. You can easily postpone the rain or snow, however, as long as you don't go near the box of bulbs. Two weeks, three weeks . . . as long as you want. Just touch the box when you want it to rain. It will. Sometimes, just for fun, it won't. Instead, it waits until you've hauled out the cart, the spade, the rake, the labels and bone-meal, and the garden map; until you've dug the necessary trench and got the box half-emptied and bulbs strewn all over the landscape . . . then it rains. Gardening *can* be a challenge.

If, by some extraordinary set of circumstances, you must be away from the garden in fall, then most likely you will have no problem with rain whatsoever. The weather will be absolutely perfect for planting bulbs, but they will not arrive, of course. At least not until the day after you leave for Kansas City. Someone, I am confident, arranges these things . . . a sort of anti-gardener you might say. They certainly do not happen by themselves. Occasionally you might find that delivery of the bulbs actually occurs the day after you return. This is a minor victory, I suppose, in this battle of the bulbs, but it will do you little good in the larger view of things. It will take you until the next weekend to get to the planting phase and by that time it will be raining. I do not make these things up, you know, they just simply are.

I routinely endure these minor setbacks, as all gardeners must, because there is one thing about the garden (and normally the weather) that will never leave us. Hope. Actually an enormous amount of hope and a little patience are the secrets of gardening. Without them we cannot manage. Take the rain, for instance, or the cold weather. It will stress our sense of duty to bulb and garden; it will cause us to worry if we care for that sort of thing, and it will cause us to mutter short words which are normally foreign to us. But just when it would seem best all around to burn the bulbs rather than let them rot, a remarkable thing happens . . . as if some kind force senses our lack of humor in this dark situation. A bulb-planting day erupts. From nowhere, it would seem, but there it is. And my advice to all of us is that when that day arrives, we'd best plant like we mean it—even if it should mean cancelling a dental appointment. We must plant with the fear of Holland in us.

We must drag out our bulb maps at this point and locate suitable places to stuff even more plant life. The little bare patches hither and yon, cracks in the garden to fill with mortar of crocus and anemone, tulip and daffodil, glory-of-the-snow, and snowdrop. The trick here, of

course, is finding the cracks without ravaging the older bulb plantings, and I'm afraid no map actually helps all that much.

The inadequacy of maps and the knowledge that garden cracks are always in the most inaccessible places, usually means not only stepping all over what little plant life still survives above ground, but also slicing a few old bulbs in half with the spade. It is probably good for them, but it always gives me a sickening feeling, somewhat as if I'd just cut a worm in half. Regardless of biological reality, I cannot believe that worms enjoy doubling in number by being sliced through the middle. They possess far better ways of increasing their numbers.

The exact location determined, we are now approximately almost nearly ready to plant next year's glory. And here we may rely on numerous methods of bulb insertion depending largely upon what sort of person we are and what sort of soil we have. If you have very good, friable soil a simple dibble or trowel is all that is required. I, on the other hand, rely mainly upon spade, fork, axe, crowbar, and dynamite.

Because most of my "garden" has been in sod for 40 years (mostly before my time) or lies in the root runs of rather vicious trees, I must always prepare my soil before planting anything. Thus a dibble is not my first choice of weaponry. My first choice would actually be a different garden, but numerous problems preclude this fantasy. One weapon I definitely cannot, nor would not, use is that little tin cooky-cutter thing they sell at garden centers. The one you insert in the ground and a plug of soil comes out; you stick the bulb in and replace the divot. Right! If you haven't cut off three fingers by the time you stick the thing in the ground, then it is probably already bent six ways of Sunday. They do make an elongated, modified version of this contraption . . . a sort of bulb-planting pogo stick as it were . . . but the stress forces make this tool virtually useless. I really can't imagine who buys this sort of gadget; it serves a very short-lived function . . . and not very well at that. A simple trowel or spade (plus the dynamite) are tool enough.

    As to the actual planting of bulbs I have few words of wisdom. As I have said before, there are many texts which tell you exactly, and in precise detail, how to dig a hole. But with bulbs you must also know how to compute its length, its correct planting depth, and how to fill the soil back into the hole again. These days, someone undoubtedly sells a computer software program (such as Bulbcomput) which may be used to tell one exactly how to do this. I doubt, however, that even a computer could tell us which direction is "up" on an anemone tuber. Not that it seems to matter much, though.

    For me, the easiest method of planting (other than dynamite) seems to be to take a spade and excavate the entire area wherein the bulbs will lie and then to pile the soil beside the hole or in the cart. Next I take the bag of bulbs and pour them gently into the hole only to find that a rather strange problem has arisen. No matter how large I've managed

to dig the hole, it is never big enough to hold the few bulbs I've put in. Never! I cannot figure out exactly how this happens, but it does, and it is irritating. I must now pick up all the poor brown things I've just dumped out, return them to the bag, and dig again. For the next set of bulbs I dig the hole even bigger, so large in fact that the entire box of bulbs should fit . . . unpacked. It won't, of course, and when I pour in the feebly small bag of crocus, even they won't fit. I've concluded, finally, that it is a sort of bulb curse . . . one that has been inherited from some evil spirit in the family. Perhaps some rakish lout who once rankled a ranunculus, or squashed a squill.

Whatever the reason, when the hole is finally correctly fitted, I have sadly reached the last stage in my battle with the bulbs. They sit forlornly ensconced at the bottom of the trench, each wrapped in its own brown paper wrapper. I roll the soil over their heads and scarcely believe these weak, unclad bits of flesh will survive the barbaric beating they are about to endure. Months of ice and snow; frozen one day and buried in mud the next . . . not much of a life it would seem . . . these victims of a gardener's skirmish. But we know that in losing the battle they have won the war. And so have we. Now, what could possibly be better than that?

15
Winters of My Discontent

Preemptive battles notwithstanding, winter does not come with the bulbs but after them. Fall merely heralds the true battle which is shortly to begin. Eventually among its crop of days one senses the lustre of these brassy calls beginning to tarnish—soon to fade entirely. It happens slowly this clouding, imperceptible to all but the wariest. And of the wary, the gardener must steadfastly guard the forefront in anticipation of fall's tottering steps as it stumbles headlong into winter's oblivion. The battle for hearts and minds is about to begin.

Much work remains to be done if the keeper is to protect his keep, and it is not entirely unexpected that he is assailed at every turn by magazine, newspaper, and nursery warning of the perils of not mulching, or of too much mulching, or of too little (depending, of course, upon the authority), of moisture, of draining pipes, of dragging this in and putting that out, of getting ready for next spring or next summer, and on and on, until the uninitiated is whirling to the tune of everyone elses' fiddle.

The practiced gardener, is oblivious to this greenbelt-hype, however, and will have breached the forefront of hysteria days before. He will be "caught-up" with the physical chores and perhaps he will be caught-up with the mental ones as well (although this is not only dangerous, but nearly impossible). But will he be caught-up emotionally? I never am.

Winter is the battleground for heart and mind, and no matter how well I might reinforce the garden I have yet to reinforce myself to winter's vicious attacks . . . to sit and do nothing as buddleias sprawl painfully to the ground, or azaleas burn in icy cold blasts, as evergreens turn to everbrowns.

Some gardeners would have you believe that they actually enjoy this sort of thing. Garden writers write chapters or even entire books on what to grow in winter. They tell us which shrubs have attractive bark, or cheerful berries, or even what will be flowering in January—there, just 3 ft. beneath the snow's surface.

My own opinion is that there are very few words at all to describe winter . . . and none of them are fit to print.

Because I am obviously a timid gardener and cannot bear to witness the wholesale onslaught of death and destruction about me, I am forced to compensate for reality by several minor adjustments in behavior. I list these behavioral modifications for those of you who might have a similar reaction to winter.

1. Do not look at the garden in winter, it is only aggravating and causes ulcers. I go to work in the dark and return home in the dark. I see nothing—and that is good. The weekends, however, pose a problem which I have yet to solve, except perhaps when I sleep through them. Glimpses are caught from time to time of the frozen pond with rocks heaving in from the sides, of flagstones and ice gnawing at the back door, or of an azalea lying on its side, its roots ripped cleanly out of the ground. The only solution is to pray for Monday.

2 (A). Pretend that you are on vacation, sit under a sun lamp, listen to reggae music, and read a fascinating gardening book. This is good for three reasons. Firstly, because doctors have shown that bright light overcomes the depression brought on by decreasing day-length. Secondly, because reading about gardening is almost as good as being there. (Don't read any of those "how-to" books, though, they are just counter-antidepressing.) Thirdly, you can catch up on your garden reading in the winter (when there is "nothing-to-do") and have more time the rest of the year to garden. In fact, if you are reading this in the spring, summer, or fall, I suggest that you put it down straightaway and get back to your garden. I don't want anyone using me as an excuse to loaf away three-quarters of the year.

2 (B). Pretend that you have lots of money, sit under a sun lamp, listen to Uruguayan pipe music, and read lots of gardening catalogs. If

you have heaps of money, of course, you don't have to pretend. The rest of us will. Obviously this is just another method of fighting depression by the power of positive spending. Everyone knows that spending money is good for the soul. Bury yourself amidst all of those free catalogs—there are tons of different sorts—and make up endless lists of seeds, new plants to try, and shrubs to buy. Remember that $5.00 worth of seeds is equal to one $50.00 visit to a psychiatrist. I have saved myself thousands of dollars in doctor bills.

3. Turn up the furnace, listen to some Estonian fiddle music, and watch the houseplants die. This is actually one of my favorite winter pastimes. I don't like houseplants as a rule, but I always seem to have an endless supply. These are usually given to me by misguided people who think that anyone who gardens outside also likes to garden inside. I don't (except see No. 7, below). Houseplants are nice, I suppose, but they're mostly just a damn nuisance. All winter long they sulk, rot, attenuate, defoliate, and dissipate in various ways. If aphids and scales don't kill them whatever you spray them with will. Water spots the carpet and stains the furniture. It takes six months outside after winter has passed to get them back to proper health just so you can bring them

inside in time to try to kill them again. (Anyone who undertakes the revitalization of the following sorts of plants should be summarily sent to Buffalo for the winter: the florist azaleas brought home from a six-week stay at Our-Mother-of-the-Sacred-Hearts Hospital; poinsettia of any color or dimension; a curiosity-bowl of cactus with various sorts of phallic succulents and hens-and-chickens; an Easter lily or bunch of tulips in a foil-wrapped pot that you were given for Mother's Day, Father's Day, children's day, grandma's day, or leper's day. All of these plants will die, and if they don't they should.)

4. Watch television, work puzzles, or play cards. These endeavors will most probably drive you entirely mad, but that is good practice. It is the norm for gardeners.

5. Drink a lot, use drugs, and party with wild members of the opposite (or same, if you prefer) sex. I admit to taking great quantities of aspirin due to excessively depressive headaches. Other than this, I cannot afford to live the life of dissoluteness, dissipation, and decadence which I would chose to live if I but had the choice.

6. Make troughs. This is a particularly English pastime and little known in the United States—rather like flonking the dyile, a game in which beer-soaked rags are hurled at participants. The British are good at this sort of thing. Making troughs involves mixing various combinations of cement, peatmoss, and pearlite to a "cheese-like" consistency and then forming it into sink-like affairs called troughs. These are merely artificial replacements for age-old stone sinks which are apparently difficult to find in Britain these days (and impossible in the United States). These containers are then distressed to appear as if carved out of stone, and they really do appear stone-like. Rock and alpine gardeners use these creations as pots for their more cherished plants. In many ways this is the English equivalent of the Japanese "saikei" or miniaturized landscape, except that the Japanese miniaturize the plants and scale whereas the English merely put an alpine outcropping and all of its plants in a big pot. (I think I may have lost something in the translation, but the thought is still correct.)

7. Start seeds in the basement. After you have followed my advice under point 2 (B), you probably will have purchased about 250 packets of seeds. Sometime in December you will want to plant these, but I advise against it ("Kitchen Garden" provides the details). Wait at least until January as I do . . . or until February if you are a confirmed masochist. There will be no need to invent things to do after the seed

start sprouting. You will be sorry, of course, that you bought so many seeds—enough, if truth be known, to carpet the entire state of New Jersey—but you won't be able to throw any seedlings away. That is against the rules.

8. Work on your paper gardens. After you've started all those seeds you'll have to look at your garden plan to figure out where to put them. Of course the more logical of you will have used a paper garden to figure out where the seeds went first, then ordered them. I cannot help this in the least; it seems entirely too organized for me.

9. Stay at work an extra 20 hours a week. I did this for two winters and it is a good way to catch up with work. Most people will not believe that federal workers (as I am) put in overtime. We do and we don't get paid a cent extra or even get comp-time (at least I don't). I gave up overtime for several good reasons, I think. Firstly, because no one appreciated the effort except me and I decided to live down to the scurrilous opinion that most people have of government workers. Secondly, because I took up writing to overcome my winter blues. There was no time to do extra at work when I could work at home. I still don't get paid much or get overtime. But it's worth it.

10. Write about things. What you write about is mostly irrelevant. I write about gardens for example, which is mostly irrelevant. I

have a friend who writes about trains—he specializes in Southern Pacific steam locomotives—which seems about as irrelevant as one can get. Yet we both have fun writing—well at least he does, it is still work for me. There is little or no money in garden writing so it is probably best regarded as therapeutic rather than lucrative. If you wish to make money at this I recommend that you become a writing dentist or veterinarian, an actor or crazed cult-leader, or an anorexic chef who writes diet books. They all seem to prosper.

*   *   *   *

In winter I do all of the above things, some with slight modifications, as well as some other things which are best left to the imagination. But my primary passion lies in the last-mentioned, namely writing. I write to overcome the season because I do not particularly enjoy it. Perhaps it is because I do not enjoy being cold, or wet, or even miserable. A real garden is not worth that sacrifice, but paper gardens whether mapped or written *do* restore at least warmth and dryness (I still tend to be slightly miserable in spite of them).

Take yesterday, for instance, and today. Yesterday I had to clean the pond, reaching elbow deep into waters that had just passed through a fortuitous thawing in early December. Five minutes spent in that environment and I was ready for a sauna (which I don't have, by the way). Yet indoors, today, I may work on my terrace, or map out a new bed of shrubs, without the least bit of discomfort (except, perhaps, for a few cat claws in the leg). I can work in spite of snow, or sleet, in spite even of gloom of day.

As I mentioned earlier, there are gardeners who revel in the winter—often making nasty little comments about those of us who hibernate for the season. (These are often the same people who have just spent the summer estivating in an air-conditioned house and who only ventured outdoors to work in the garden when it was safe.) These are the gardeners and writers who are full of colorful bark, christmas roses, stark, ethereal patterns (as of fountain grass against the yews), ever-so-pretty berries, and mostly various forms of hot gases. If they wish to enliven their lives with these masochistic deceptions I say let them. But pray do not lull me into the garden with your sadistic little tricks—for I fall all-too-easily a victim to the whims of others. Even when they are wrong.

Now there are those who honestly tell me they enjoy winter because it gives them a break from the heavy labor of spring, summer, and fall. I used to believe this line of twisted reasoning, but actually I think they are just a little mixed up. It is only the fact that they can't garden that makes them accept the sour (and frozen) grapes of winter. If summer continued forever so would they and you would not hear the false prophets of rest and relaxation.

But I fear, perhaps, that I am taking a rather bleak case of the winter blahs and becoming quite infectious with it. Lest I have begun to stir the deep-seated anxieties or depressions in your own breast I had better recommend that you return to "Summer Thoughts" (Chapter 13) or that I end winter's curse with a cheery little story about daffodils. (The editor tells me that unless I brighten up the mood a bit you will throw this book down and sulk for the remainder of the winter—hence the daffodils.)

It cannot be particularly easy to be a plant even under the best of circumstances, especially if you are a bulb. I have tried to place myself in a bulb's position, and I cannot really see the advantage in it (plus it hurts my back a great deal when I try to curl up tightly in a paper bag—which is, after all, what a bulb is if you care to think about those sorts of things).

One year, after performing all of my necessary bulb duties, I was forced to leave the garden for a lengthy period of time. To my dismay I discovered that during my absence a new sewer line was to be run down

the street. To do this they would have to remove the new picket fence I had just built, but more to the point they would be using my newly planted bulb bed as a race track for tractors. I could do nothing, and such is my constitution that I was glad I could see nothing as well.

My return home in March merely confirmed the fact that I was glad not to have been there during most of the construction. My bulb bed was a sea of mud formed into frozen, tire-marked waves of amber. It was truly a sight to behold, and not one likely to be shown in the books that tell "how splendid a winter garden can be." But I could do nothing—they were not yet finished destructing the street—so that's what I did. (As you can see, there are good points to disasters, too.)

Instead, I watched the mud. I don't know why, perhaps I am a closet optimist. It was inconceivable that anything had been left in the soil (the excavation was to 15 ft) let alone survive to sprout, or even more amazingly to bloom. And yet something did. Two somethings as a matter of fact.

One was a cubic-foot clod of clay which had been dug up for some reason and pitched onto a pile of dirt. From the sides of this clod there began to emerge the tips of tulips—horizontal at first, but then straightening to gain the sun as best they could. They bloomed some-how, but just barely. It was a statement of intent really and not much more.

Nearby, however, a flock of the daffodil 'February Gold' was beginning to emerge from the mud as if nothing much had actually happened. The fact that it was two months late, here in mid-April, just proved that it was holding its own until the trucks backed off. After being frozen solid for weeks on end, after resting in semi-liquid soil for endless days, after being run over repeatedly by heavy road destruc-tion equipment, *and* after having mounds of compacted mud casually tossed on top of it, 'February Gold' had inched its way up and proclaimed its intention to survive.

It was not extremely pretty, sitting there in the mud. Not the sort of thing you'd see in *Horticulture* magazine to be certain. Its flowers were battered from the wind and rain—supplicant to the ground and caked with soil—kicked as a few oafmen cleaned up the last of the roadwork. After twelve weeks of winter it was not a pretty sight at all—but deter-mined as hell.

I know exactly how those daffodils feel, too, after the winters of *my* discontent.

16
Kitchen Garden

Why is it, do you suppose that stovetops aren't made large enough to support more than two flats of plants at a time? Or refrigerators more than one? If someone ever builds a six-flat stove I would certainly buy one, but in the meantime I must make do with only the two flats on top. I really shouldn't complain, I suppose, because I can arrange one additional flat in the oven, but this is never quite as satisfactory as it might appear (as, for example, when one absent-mindedly preheats the oven). The dishwasher is completely out of the question, of course, as it is normally full of Bruno's food, and he would become quite rude if I were to move the cans of tuna and mackerel to some other place. But that is just the problem, you see, if builders only made kitchens large enough to hold the extra half-dozen or so flats we wouldn't need to put the cat's food in the dishwasher. There could be enough space for everything.

Perhaps it would be wise to explain why the situation in the kitchen has become so critical. It isn't that it is so terribly small, mind you, I mean there is room for a pot, a plate, and a fork which are about the correct number of essential tools for life. And there is a proper sink, refrigerator, stove, and dishwasher which serve their primary purpose of supporting flats. And Bruno even has room to turn around if he balances just right on his hind legs. No, you can't say the kitchen is too small. *It* is not actually the problem. Rather, the problem seems to lie somewhere between the basement and the last day of frost. Of the latter

I will say more in a moment, but I should start more properly at the beginning if this is going to make any sense at all.

The basement is the root of my problems, you might say, for it is here, sometime in January's miserable clutches, that the urge to garden begins to break its winter dormancy. It has been weeks (in most years, anyway) since the last outdoor work was finished. Months, at least, since the last green shoots were charred black by the frost. And it will be years (or so it seems) before the garden will be starting up again. Yet somehow the gardener's nervous system knows it is just about the right time to muster seed packets to the fore. It might be some magnetic pull on the brain cells or some innate response to a microscopic increase in day length. Then again it may just be seed-sellers' hype. Whatever it is, seeds attain a grip on our psyche and they must be served.

So out they come from the freezer, from the used margarine tubs, from the sandwich bags, out they must come to be ranked and filed according to the gardener's litany: heights and spreads must be noted (shorties to the front), times of bloom calculated, colors synchronized (do they ever?), sun or shade plotted (usually between), seed treatment ascertained (nick, file, soak, freeze, boil, burn, roast, toast), seed soil treatment needed (capers, everyone knows, must have cement added to the seed pots for proper germination). And on it goes until each packet is organized into a pile according to its proper lot in life and the time at which it is to be officially started. These are then marked with a date and stacked in readiness for such time as the rituals shall begin.

At first it is easy, this starting business. A few pots, planted up just after New Year's, watered down, put in a plastic bag, and placed outside to be harassed for weeks on end by a belligerent winter climate. Perhaps I should have said easy for the gardener; it wouldn't seem to be so easy to be a seed. But actually many seeds are masochistic little devils and love the rigors of all this freezing and thawing business. They are welcome to it, I say, as I work in my warm basement potting up a few of the more intelligent seeds, as we might call them. These are the ones which appreciate a warm, moist spot with lots of light . . . much as any right-thinking sort might do.

For several weeks now, since I'd first put those barbarian sorts out to freeze their little seed-coats off, the number of seed pots in my basement has been quite respectable. In fact the basement seemed rather bare; a few pots under a light and that was that. I am absolutely in total command of the situation. It is, as we might say, an idealist's paradise. Then, without so much as a minute's warning, the trouble starts. The number of seed pots begins to double on a weekly basis, and the number of transplants begins to grow exponentially. On go all of the lights and timers, seed pots which haven't sprouted are banished to some darkened corner until they prove the need for light. Excess seedlings which last week might have been tenderly potted up, now start to hit the composting box with terrifying frequency.

And then it begins in earnest, the inexorable movement of green things up the stairs. First in six-packs on the counters. Then a flat or two on the stove. The refrigerator soon follows and then even the floor. Relatively quickly the kitchen surrenders all of its space and it's on to the dining room table. By now the situation has become both better and worse: better because a few of the hardier things can be banished to the screened porch, worse because I usually put out all of the tender things as well. It just seems the thing to do. I mean I'm already eating dinner off

the arm of the sofa; one must retain some pride. . . . mustn't one?

So here I am then, flats flung over the kitchen, flats floundering on the porch, flats flooding the basement, and I still await the day which will cure all of my problems, that most mystical of all gardening days: the last day of frost. If ever a person should receive the grand prize for all of gardening it would have to be that person who could pinpoint the last day of frost to within, say, three days, or even a week.

In my region, usually referred to as Zone 6 but actually some incalculable and changeable decimal between 5 and 7, our average dates of last frost are something on the order of 30 March to 30 April. But this is only average, of course, so another week or two might be added for absolute safety. Thus we have a choice of about four to six weeks of "last day of frost" by which to reckon our previous planting dates. And as we all know, the seed packets tell us to plant, for example, eight weeks before the last frost. It does not take a computer to figure out that one can be off as much as six weeks if things go badly. And in any case it won't matter a whit even if things should go superbly because you won't know it until the six weeks have passed anyway . . . by which time the entire matter is irrelevant: the plants have already taken over everything.

Last days and all not withstanding, I am still left with the problem of what to do with all those flats. And I am stuck with this problem until such time as the last frost should manage to strike. It is well to remember this fact, and I most certainly always do when, at 6:45 in the morning, I walk onto the porch to find death and destruction all about. Of course I was just off to work, but that must wait. With great pangs of grief I rush all about trying to revive the near-dead and dead alike. Maybe a little warm water or a kind word or two. If luck has its way perhaps only half of the tender things are beyond hope. I try to think such positive thoughts as I drive off to work. From now on I shall have to bring these battle-scarred survivors in every evening . . . just to be certain. And so begins the juggling of flats, the tender things to the stove for the night, the half-hardies covered with inverted flats, and the stronger things just take what they get. Sorry, there's no more room in the kitchen.

17
Not Gardens
(Or manmade follies
and other natural disasters)

It does not take much experience in the garden to learn that weeds and foolishness grow rampantly. Often this foolishness is of our very own making, but on occasion we have much needed help from our friends or neighbors. Usually, however, it comes from a source as yet unspecified, relegated to the nether regions of cosmic instability. (At least in-so-far as I can determine.) All of which is to say that gardens have a mind of their own and are not always precisely in tune with our own.

Who amongst us has not planted out some tender young thing of great desirability wishing that it would overwinter in Zone 6 and knowing that it wouldn't? Or a primrose where it is too dry? We try these things because we want them to work or we hope they will work and we will gladly risk the disappointment if they don't. In the real world these are referred to as experiments and are looked upon as necessities for the advancement of humankind. In the garden such things are called foolishness (if the gardener does it on purpose) or ignorance (if it is done by mistake). Occasionally, when the gardener has no control whatsoever it is called a disaster.

I. OF ECHIUMS AND IGNORANCE

I once tried to grow *Echium fastuosum* and discovered that not only would it not grow in my garden but it was not even the plant I wanted to grow—exactly. But I suppose I should begin at the beginning as the whole affair gets rather complicated towards the end and the middle is not entirely simple either.

In the beginning I was a Californian as I have said, and there is not much anyone can do about that. It happens. The fact that I was born in Washington, D.C. has little to do with this particular story, but is historically accurate. I moved to San Francisco at such an early age that I was unaware at the time, but I do recall having an adverse reaction to politicians . . . a rash, I think. Later in my life, when I had a choice, I returned to Washington. The rash is much worse.

As I said, being a Californian by adoption, and being used to a mediterranean climate, I have had great difficulty adjusting to the east and its totally unpredictable weather. Even more aggravating has been having to learn to garden all over again. Somehow it does not seem fair, and it isn't, but that seems to be irrelevant. What *is* relevant is that practically everything I did in the beginning was oriented towards recalling the way things were and trying to make them that way here.

Once, not too awfully many years ago, I returned to the West and was quickly overcome by an unfamiliar plant I saw growing at the side of my parent's house. Actually there were two plants, both the same kind, one about a foot high and looking all the world like a rosette of rabbit's ears sticking straight out, and the other about 5 ft. high, shaped a little like a narrow Christmas tree with the upper two-thirds covered in bluish purple flowers. It was the sort of thing one dreams about (. . . well sometimes at least). My mother had obtained the plants at some church sale or other for about 35¢. She didn't know what they were and neither did anyone else. No one ever seems to know what these mysterious sorts of plants are—the kind that grandma gets at a neighborhood flea-market, plants next to the garden gate, and three weeks later there arises an 8 ft. tall, bedazzling tower of a plant that might as well have come from the moon for all anyone can tell.

No one seemed to know much of anything about the particular plant that grew at my mother's house except that such an one had not been seen before. Which sounds mighty strange if you ask me—it had to have come from somewhere and I wanted one!

Several years passed as I asked around of anyone who would listen about a plant which was becoming more and more like a religious experience in my memory. But finally I discovered a clue somewhere . . . I can't recall from where, right now, but somewhere apparently not too striking . . . a clue of something like "crown jewels" or "tower-of-crowns" or some such name. And from that name I worked my way through the literature to a genus called *Echium*.

I read up on the genus as best as I could, but there doesn't seem to be a large amount written about it and I didn't find exactly what I needed to know. I ended up investing in some seed of *Echium fastuosum* because it was the only commonly available, non-annual seed I could find, and because the picture of the flower in the seed catalog looked about as I recalled the plant ought to look. There were, however, two slight discrepancies between the information I knew about the "real" plant and the seed of the one that I was about to grow. The first was that *E. fastuosum* was a half-hardy perennial and the plant I wanted was almost certainly a biennial. The second was that the plant I wanted had a common name with "jewels" or "tower" in it, but *E. fastuosum* was called "shrubby viper's bugloss." Common names notwithstanding, it doesn't seem likely to me that the two would be easily confused!

As I implied earlier in this chapter, my experiences with these echiums were designed to be experimental, not particularly ignoramical as they seem to have become by this point. However there is some hope for me, I feel, if you can continue along just a bit further.

All of these echiums are supposed to be annual or half-hardy perennials for warmish-type climates (like coastal California). The one my mother grew appeared to be biennial, and I had hopes of taking advantage of this fact in the winter-frigid east. I was going to pamper the plant along the first year in a large pot, overwintered indoors, and then plant it out early in the second year. It seems like an unreasonable amount of work, I know, but some plants are worth it at least once in a lifetime.

Well, to make a dull story short, I grew *E. fastuosum* on through the first year as I'd planned. But by the end of that year I absolutely knew I was growing the wrong plant because of a trip I took back to the homeland where I saw this species blooming all about the place. I even saw it in a garden that I had helped tend for nearly 10 years without knowing that *that* was what you called the thing.

It is a magnificent plant to be certain; a shrub of about 3–4 ft. in height which puts out candelabras of flowers for another 2–3 ft. Probably too common to be appreciated in its own home, this echium is especially attractive poking its spears over a grape-stake or picket fence, or on a bank about shoulder high.

My own seedlings, I decided ruthlessly would have to go outside the first winter, first because I had no room to pamper these imposters forever in pots in the house (they were shrubby perennials, remember, not the biennials I had hoped to find), and secondly, because I thought it was worth a try to see what would happen outdoors. Gardeners are always talking about micro-climates and warm pockets in the garden—perhaps if I planted them over the septic tank they would be warm enough. They weren't of course, and died with great alacrity after about the fifth killer frost.

But this does not end the search for my fabled mystery plant. By no means. As a matter of fact I believe I have discovered the truth about this entire little story and I may yet prove that such a plant can be grown in the harsh eastern climate. While reading through Everett's recently published *Encyclopedia of Horticulture* (The New York Botanical Garden, 1983) I discovered that there is a species of *Echium* called *pininana* and its common name is "tower-of-jewels." It blooms once at the end of its second year and dies. It has a broad rosette of hirsute, grey leaves, and a height of 6–15 ft. It blooms as a tower of purple-blue flowers, and it hybridizes with *E. fastuosum* to produce an intermediate form of especial horticultural interest in the San Francisco bay region. I do not make this up. This hybrid has got to be the plant I am searching for, and I am taking steps this very evening to get the seeds and find out.

We gardeners may be an ignorant lot to some, but no one can fault us for our determination.

II. DYDYMUS' FOLLY

Gardeners are a peculiar lot and our reasons for "doing things" are, as often as not, about as sensible as war. In fact most of the time we are without reason entirely and therefore differ little from politicians. I need go no further than my "Knot Garden" to prove this point to everyone's satisfaction.

Why anyone, myself included, should want to grow such a labor-intensive geegaw is quite beyond me. But I planted one once, and I must have had a very good reason for it or I would not have done so. The reason, however, now escapes me entirely, which is probably best for everyone concerned . . . especially me. It was a semi-abject failure from the start and a perfect example of how to not garden.

Knot gardens have been with us a long while, if we may believe history, having originated in the Middle Ages and peaking in intensity during the 1500's. Simply put, knots were designs set out in clipped, low-growing plants of the time. They were of two sorts: 1) closed, the design being like that in a coloring book with single blocks of colored flowers filling up the spaces, or 2) open, without plants filling in the spaces. One theory has it that knots were developed as points of interest in the garden owing to the poverty of ornamental flowers.

My own interest in such things began with exposure to a book entitled *Medieval Gardens* by Frank Crisp. This book contains over 500 illustrations of gardens from the Middle Ages and I thought some of the ideas seemed both simple and intriguing. Perhaps I could duplicate one of the designs using original plants and thus create a bit of history in my own garden.

After scouring the numerous illustrations for some time, I decided to try the most simple design in the book. This consisted essentially of a square inside of a circle with four ovals radiating from the center like the petals of a daisy. It was a design from *The Gardeners' Labrinth* by Dydymus Mountaine published in 1571. Now here, I thought at the time, was seriously, scholarly stuff, and I christened my venture "Dydymus' Folly." [I later learned that this design seems to be very common among knotists, and the Time-Life Book of Herbs (1977) not only features a picture of the knot on its cover but also explains exactly how to lay it out. According to this source, the knot is patterned on one which dates from about the reign of Elizabeth I at Hampton Court, England.]

Next came the choice of plants with which I would create the knot. These would have to be plants "authentic" to the time, of which box, rosemary, hyssop, thyme, lavender, lavender cotton, germander, gillyflower, or thrift were but a few. Several sorts were eliminated immediately. In the case of box, for example, I did not have the necessary life-span nor patience to imagine what the finished result might look like; nor did I have a few thousand dollars to purchase plants large enough to do the job. Rosemary would have been my first choice because it is a good bee-plant. Unfortunately it is not hardy in my area. Gillyflower was out because I couldn't imagine any form of the plant that would be the least bit suitable for upright, clipped hedges, and I doubted that the current readily obtainable carnations would be anything like their predecessors. Thrift posed the same sort of structural problem.

Of the remaining plants, I decided to use what I could find "in the trade" only to find that I couldn't find what I was looking for, or rather more importantly, I couldn't find anything that I could afford. Rough figuring demonstrated that I needed at least 150 plants to make the pattern 10 ft. in diameter, and even at the ridiculously low figure of $2.00 per plant that is a lot of money for a square, a circle, and some daisy petals. The only recourse left, of course, was to grow them from seed. And since I was growing them from seed, which was quite a rational way to go about things, and I was not so severely limited to readily available plants, I decided to make each shape of the knot from a different type of plant. No sense being totally monotonous about it.

So I pored though the seed catalogs and descriptions of suitable plant species, and I did one other thing . . . I read up on the medieval uses of these plants just to see if there might be some practical byproduct to all of this. After all, I would be clipping the hedges routinely to keep them neat (this was specified in my papers of indenture), and perhaps I could sell off the excess to my local potpourrist, herbalist, or all else failing, witch. Maybe this folly might even pay for itself in the end. One must be ever resourceful in the garden . . . even a nouveau-medieval one . . . that is the gardening spirit!

After taking into account all conceivable factors such as availability, hardiness, color, cost, and access to local witches, I made three choices for the knot components. The first was "lavyndull" (*Lavendula vera*) which I used for the inner square. This is a soft gray-foliaged plant whose excess leaves can be used to "perfume linnen, apparel, gloues, leather, &c.," whose flowers can be dried "to comfort and dry up the moisture of a cold braine," and whose "oyle" can be used for "old and benummed parts." It sounded to me as if I had discovered something here . . . I mean benummed parts and cold brains are legion in my area . . . 20 miles from the nation's capital.

Second on my list of choices came lavender cotton (*Santolina chamaecyparissus*) for the "daisy petals." This is a lighter shade of gray and has open, lacey foliage rather than the upright foliage of lavender. When clipped its excesses could properly be used in "bathes," as "ointments for cold causes," and its seeds used "for the wormes." Yes, indeedy I was beginning to feel like a regular apothecary right here in my own physic garden.

And for the final choice to be used as the circle I selected hyssope (*Hyssopus officialis*) a dark, sepulchral green which would contrast with the gray of the square within it and the ovals which passed through it. Concoctions of hyssope essence could be used as "an oyle made of the herbe and flowers" which "doth comfort benummed sinews and joynts," and it could be taken as "drinkes, to help to expectorate flegme."

Those were serious times—the Middle Ages—what with so much benummed parts, cold braines, and excess flegme. You have to wonder just how our race actually made it to the Renaissance. But unfortunately it did and that is too bad really for all concerned.

Seeds of lavender and *Hyssopus* were planted in February in my basement which were joined in March by the lavender cotton. Germination of each was complete in three weeks time and the

Rosemary
Sage, Yarrow
Tansey, lavender,
Hyssop

seedlings were pricked out and placed into market packs. By early May some of the transplants had already begun to fill out the knot, and with the aid of strings and stakes the planting was completed in early June with a total of 157 plants.

The actual growing and planting part probably sounds reasonably simple on the surface and, for the purpose of this little exercise, it was. But that is only because I have essentially told you the story of both elsewhere: the growing pains in *Kitchen Garden* and the parable of the digging in *Greengrocers*. As you may recall, though I seriously doubt it, we went through a very long discourse on the preparation of certain vegetable beds at the base of a certain silver maple tree. It happens that this bed was constructed on the left side of the tree, which by all sorts of algebraic figuring left the area on the right side of the tree available for other forms of madness.

I need not go into the frustration of digging yet again, but let us just say that the right area under the tree differed remarkably little from the left. There were the prerequisite number of nails, spark plugs, rocks, and, of course, tree roots. It is somewhat to my credit that I actually began soil preparation for the knot garden one year in advance of planting. Conversely, I suppose, it is not to my credit that I failed to finish.

My original goal had been to make the knot garden the center of a small (25' × 20') courtyard which was surrounded on three sides by a hedge. Thus the knot would form the center of a hidden medieval garden which would suddenly appear as one walked through, or around, the hedge. I had planted the hedge several years in advance, based upon my garden plans, so it was beginning to fill in. Still, 500 sq. ft. of turf removal, tree root removal, and preparation by hand is a bit of a task and I hadn't finished the entire area.

Enough was excavated and cleared, however, to put in the knot, which I did. The rest would have to wait until I got around to it, as they say. Fortunately I didn't need to get around to it, for in the end I changed the entire project and abandoned the knot garden.

It is better, I suppose, to recognize that one has made a mistake (or two) and to suffer the consequences in as grown-up a manner as one might manage. In this respect we would do well to learn from such bastions of suavity as our feline friends. When they have done something obviously stupid (which they do on rare occasion) and they know you are watching, they pretend as if they really meant to do that stupid thing on purpose . . . as if to amuse the humans who might be lurking about. If no one should be lurking about, of course, they turn their back on such a matter and believe it never really happened.

Unfortunately we human sorts do not have it quite so easy. Our mistakes are usually all too obvious . . . especially when they are 10 ft. square . . . and we suffer immeasurably from guilt. The knot garden, I must admit in all candor, might have been rightly thought out, properly researched, and perhaps even expertly grown, but it certainly was built in the absolutely wrong place. I tried to rationalize the entire concept to myself as I went along, and it *did* make sense to me, after all. I mean herbs do like to grow in dry, impoverished soil. Hadn't Bradley admonished in his book of 1739 (*New Improvements of Planting and Gardening, both Philosophical and Practical*) that lavender is "apt to suffer . . . especially if they have too much wet, and therefore should be planted in chiefly the dryest Parts of the *Garden*." And I had done just that. It was certainly dry and impoverished under that silver maple. Except, of course, in the spring when it was more like the river Thames in that particular reach of the garden.

Unfortunately rationality has little place in the garden, and any amount I might have scared up at the time was of no use whatsoever in comparison to reality. And the reality was that herbs, although prospering on neglect in the sun, do not prosper at all in the shade. They merely turn spindly, spotty, and spineless as mine had done. Then, too, they probably also would object to the competition from tree roots if they'd had the energy. But they didn't. They just sulked for two years; the hyssop died out of some mysterious withering factor, while a few lavender and lavender cotton still survive to this day. I grubbed out most of them and began immediately to restructure what was to be a historical garden into my next, and much better thought out idea, which was . . .

But no! I think I'd best wait and get this one done correctly, lest I give you the impression that gardeners do not necessarily always know what they are doing.

III. NATURE'S FOLLY

Often, gardeners may succeed in spite of themselves. That is to say, we sometimes do something—perhaps even correctly—and it works. We certainly don't know why, nor is there any reason that it should have worked. But it does, and it won't happen again, so it is best to celebrate these victories with all due speed. I have never, personally, suffered such a victory, or perhaps I have been too ignorant to recognize it. But if I had had reason to celebrate, it would have been done right here in words. Instead, I make the above point to assure you that gardeners have victories and they have losses ... sometimes the victories are undeserved, and sometimes the losses are well deserved, as in my knot garden. But sometimes we have absolutely no control at all whatsoever over anything, and if this should become the case it is best not to dwell on the problem but to move onwards in the garden and ignore the source of irritation. I shall demonstrate what I mean.

By the end of my second fall in the garden I had done little else than construct an aborted rice paddy and to keep the enormous lawn under control. Mow, mow, mow, that was all I did in summer from one edge of the property to the other. Then in early fall it was rake, rake, rake—leaves—from one edge of the property to the other. At the time I had three large, venerable apple trees (one upwards of 75 years), which dumped organic material in immense quantity over everything in sight. Additionally there was the towering silver maple, the tulip poplar, and the decrepit willow in the throes of senility, not to mention a fencerow of mulberry, wild cherry, beech, and numerous other deciduous things. Enough, in all, to keep a rake perpetually flying, and a brain particularly benummed.

Amidst the green of summer and the brown of fall I had begun to long for a bed of flowers. Well, actually, not *just* a bed of flowers ... that would have been too easy. It had to be an English bed of flowers. The reason for this desire is a complicated one, I suppose, and probably a very personal one too. But it need not be discussed at this time. Suffice to say, that an English border is the first thing I shall expect to see if ever I attain St. Peter's fabled gates. If, however, I am presented with the alternative course, as is the more likely prospect, I will undoubtedly be greeted by a replica of my first two years at "English gardening." That is how pitiful my efforts were. Pitiful, but not entirely by my own making. Earnestness in gardening, however, and even diligent learning by one's own mistakes, is no match for a natural order intent on canceling classes.

My first border was drawn up during the second winter of my discontent. There were snows on top of snows that winter and it was not exactly what a Californian, recently transplanted from Florida, had learned to expect. I began this book in that winter, in fact, to allow myself to garden during this Eastern "off" season. There was nothing else to do, after all, except work 60 hours a week at my job and wish for spring's rapid arrival. So with paper and pencil, books and catalogs, and a complete disregard for reality, I planned out my border.

As the plot was in full sun every time I looked at it, I naturally planned out a "sun garden," and was naturally entirely incorrect. This case is merely a repetition of the knot garden, and does not bear additional reams of exposition. The point is, however, that by the end of the next spring, when all those bare trees had retrieved their leaves, I suddenly found I had a shade garden.

This brings us to an extremely basic point about gardening, and one that not even I will dispute until later, namely that we must respect the physical factors of our garden . . . light and shade, wet and dry, rock and clay, and so forth. However, respect in and of itself does not guarantee us any special favors in the scheme of things. It just means we may have a better chance of success if we plan things correctly. Unfortunately, such conventions do not usually help me.

Returning from principles to practicals, I found I had created a sun garden in the semi-shade. This was certainly no great tragedy . . . no cause for silent whimpering, or even kicking the cat . . . it was merely a cause for serious rethinking. So out came many of the plants, most of the daylilies, the rudbeckias of several sorts, echinaceas, heleniums, heliopsis, and potentillas, and the next spring in went the astilbes, ligularias, trollius, herbaceous anemones, and hardy cyclamen. Since the previous year I had been growing on a large number of yellow polyanthus from seed and I decided to plant these out as tidy clusters near the base of one of the large apple trees that shaded the border.

Things begin to get a bit complicated at this point, but I do distinctly remember the primulas. They were blooming nicely at the time, and actually looked as if they might be enjoying themselves. I must admit, however, that these were the first plants grown from seed in the new garden, and my exact perception of reality might have been slightly colored (or perhaps miscolored) at this point in time. There were several dozen plants in all when I left one morning for work. When I arrived home, that evening, there were scarcely any . . . well any to speak of, that is. Instead, there was a sort of primula mash, you might say, as if someone had in mind to attempt some tissue culture with a baseball bat.

Sometime during the day, the very aged apple next to the porch had split apart, and a rather hefty trunk had grazed the porch (removing its overhang), had so pulverized the primulas as to make them mad, and then had rolled over onto the top of my small automobile. The trunk had also bashed-in its neighboring apple tree so that a veritable mayhem of greenery lay strewn all about the front of my house and driveway. This, I might add, is not what one wishes to come home to after a hard day's work.

As if the tree hadn't been quite traumatic enough for the primroses, the treemen who cut down the remaining trunks and cleared up the mess, left no survivor untrodden. When finally I dared look at that planting, it had gained yet one more degree of adversity . . . it now stood in full, midday sun and the primroses were baking very nicely, thank you.

Now that I mention it, so was everything else in the shade garden. Actually I mean the sun garden. I mean, I mean . . . well, by now I don't know what I mean. The human mind can plan only so far and can adapt to only so little. Then it simply revolts . . . and my mind was revolting to say the least. My shade plants were ill-adapted to this sudden change of events, so out came the shovel once more and I moved what could be moved. Included was a single, scared primrose which is still with me today. Surprisingly it is planted beneath the limbs of yet another apple tree and shows its embattled defiance each spring with a grand round of flowers.

As for the fate of that particular part of the garden, which I have come to associate with disaster, I have sagely followed my own advice . . . do not dwell on the imponderable but move ever onwards in the garden. Even had I taken great pains to redesign that area it would all have been for naught. For as I write, plans have been approved to lay sewer pipe precisely through the middle of the bed (lengthwise, of course). I am reminded evermore that we gardeners may plan, we may scheme, we may even learn a thing or three, but we are grossly misguided if we ever think that we "have things under control."

18
Call it by Some Better Name

Entirely too much fuss is made about plant names. And here I am not referring to that rusty-gate of a debate about scientific versus common names—a much overdone subject. Authors always point out how universal and utterly precise scientific names are, yet how often we forget that a wrong name by any other name is still wrong.

To illustrate my point, I begin with an ugly, but entirely true story. I would not tell this tale except that my reputation for names is growing rampantly worse as each season turns, and it will probably do no harm to confess one of my few gardening sins.

Once I purchased seed of the choice alpine *Campanula waldsteiniana* from a choice seed house and, I might add, at a choice price. I planted the seed expecting at most one or two to germinate, but within days the pot was covered in growth as exuberant as any mustard field could muster. Overly impressed with my abilities as a sprouter of rare seed, I potted up numerous plants, labelled each pot with the scientific name (of course), and took them to the annual plant exchange of Our-Local-Chapter of The American Rock Garden Society. Things haven't been the same since.

I also planted out a few of these wondrous jewels in my fledgling rock garden. Within a week the plants had reached their described mature height of 4 in., and I began to have a rather peculiar feeling. At 12 in. I quietly dug up the harebells and moved them to an unused corner of the garden—quarantined until I could better assess the situation.

At about 5 ft. the first flowers began to open. They were very attractive, I must admit—but the scale was simply not right for an alpine plant. Anxious to know what had gone awry, I uprooted an entire plant (I had far too many anyway), folded it in thirds, and took it to a colleague in the botany department of the Smithsonian Institution.

"*Campanula rapunculoides*," he proclaimed. "A weed. Better get it out of the garden before you can't."

But I didn't, and I'm glad. I left a clump of it behind a wisteria standard where it grows easily each year in spite of its annual whack-back with the spade. Farrer referred to this campanula as the "most insatiable and irrepressible of beautiful weeds." But I've often wondered just how my rock-gardening colleagues reacted to this "jack-in-the-beanstalk" amongst the miniature glades of their rockeries. I've never had the courage to tell them who brought it. I hope they will at last understand.

This is a case, pure and simple, of an inappropriate scientific name being given to commercially produced seed. I do not claim this happens often, probably it doesn't—but it happens.

Imagine what might be the case, then, when the plant societies send out their annual lists of seed. These seed are collected and named by the members either from wild-growing natives or from the confines of cultivated gardens. Hundreds of thousands of such seed are packeted and distributed by hundreds of dedicated gardeners. What is truly amazing is not that one might end up raising a miscreant species or two, but that one ends up growing so many things that at least come close to what they are supposed to be.

Confusion of names is not confined merely to seed, by any means, although that *is* as good a place as any to begin. Once, from a highly (over)rated mail-order firm, I purchased a plant of *Sambucus racemosa* 'Plumosa Aurea.' I had seen this mound of feathery yellow leaves in England and thought it a tremendously handsome plant. You know the sort—one that I *"just-had-to-have."*

It took about six months to locate a source and secure the plant neatly in the garden, where it sat for quite a while, as bare-branched as it had arrived. Eventually it put out a few of the most ordinary, dull green leaves that could be imagined. At first I thought it might be a *Viburnum*, but then a few clusters of lavender flowers emerged and I thought it could be a *Spiraea*. Finally it produced bunches of the most incipient vile-purple berries, and I knew it was a mistake.

The firm from whom I had ordered the shrub informed me (after submission of a botanical specimen) that I had a *Callicarpa* and they replaced it with my *Sambucus*. Or rather I replaced it, after all I had to remove the old one and put the other in its place. I lost only the one year's growth, and gained two plants for the single price, but I'm not certain it was worth it. I don't really want the beautyberry as it is commonly called (talk about misguided names), and I still don't know what to do with it.

A few misnamed plants here or there actually are of little consequence to anyone except an avid nameophile, as I tend to be. True, one does waste a lot of time finding and cultivating the "wrong" plant, especially if one is aiming towards a specific landscape effect. But still it doesn't really cause a "stir," as it were, unless you inundate your peers' rockeries with 5 ft. aeonian harebells, as I am wont to do. Or unless one applies the incorrect name to a *Sternbergia* in the presence of one's peers, as I am wont to do. Then it is just plain embarrassing.

In my youth I had always coveted a small space between some flagstones in a garden I tended. Not much of a space, nor seemingly

149

much to covet, but one which erupted each fall with a bucket of golden cups. This remarkable display was named *Sternbergia lutea,* and I knew that eventually I would have to have some.

In my present garden I planted three dozen bulbs of *S. lutea* (from two different growers), and grew an entirely different appearing species. The *lutea* of my youth bloomed on stems above its leaves, whilst the latter *lutea* bloomed without its leaves and the flowers came directly from the ground.

I was attending another meeting of the aforementioned rock garden society—a meeting in a member's garden—when I spied several incredibly large patches of the *Sternbergia lutea* I had known from earlier times. I asked several very knowledgeable members if they knew the name of this *Sternbergia* and they told me it was *lutea.*

"But," I ventured with some hesitation, "this is not the *lutea* I grow."

Whereupon I was treated to some sideways glances and assorted mutterings about how many species of "*lutea* could there be."

I couldn't answer then, but I can now. There can be as many "species" of *lutea* as there are people who misidentify them and/or sell them. I finally convinced myself that the "lutea" I grow is probably *clusiana.* Regardless of what mine is, actually, I don't care that much for it, and I shall try to get the real "lutea" or even a false one, so long as it looks like the "lutea" I really want.

If some of this sounds a trifle confusing I should explain that it actually really is. I can say this because I am by profession a taxonomist—simply put, a namer of things. That I name insects (more precisely wasps, if you must know), and not plants, should not be held against me. It is only the principle of the names that is of primary interest. And it is the principles which I shall try to avoid at all costs, first because they are incredibly dull to the layman and second because they become even duller when you know something about them. Let us just say that there are rules about names and books on how to name things and then go on to the names themselves. It will be better for both of us.

As I've tried to illustrate by the foregoing comments, a scientific name can, at times, be just about as misleading as a common one. Either can be used badly, but the application of an incorrect scientific name, I think, is the more serious offense because one *assumes* such a name to be inviolately precise. Names, however, are only as accurate as their users make them.

There is another category of names, however, which is particularly awful to deal with, especially as these names fall squarely between the cracks of ordinary scientific names and ordinary common names. These are the "cultivar" (sometimes called "variety") names given to clones of genetically identical individuals. For example, rhododendron 'Fred' or chrysanthemum 'Old Bucket of Guts' (for a particularly good red form) would be examples of cultivar names. When registered with the proper authority these names, although common sounding, become semi-sort-of scientific names which are used by everyone, or nearly everyone, or at least someone who wants to sell you a plant with a different name than the one you already have.

Take, for instance, tulips. Renowned since the 1500's as the prima donna of the world of plant high-finances, cultivated tulips are so confused botanically that they have been termed "a headache for the botanist" by Brian Mathew author of *Dwarf Bulbs* (1973, B. T. Batsford, London). But whereas the botanist has a mere 50 to 150 species to worry about, the gardener must concern himself with about 3000 registered cultivar names (according to the Royal General Bulbgrowers Society, The Netherlands). True, the number drops to a few hundred in the current bulb catalogs, but it is still enough to make you wonder who needs so many tulips. Around here all one sees are red and yellow ones anyway, so who plants all the damn things?

I grow very few tulips myself, not necessarily because of the name problem, but because they seem too much work for the reward. I'm certain this point is arguable, and I'm equally certain I won't argue. It is my garden, after all, and if I don't want to fuss with tulips I won't. But I do like to fuss with *Dianthus* so I will make a few comments about them.

Dianthus is a genus of some 300 species, and if tulips might be termed a botanical "headache" then dianthus are positively a botanical "nightmare." The species interbreed rather freely, you see, and while this is probably most pleasant for them, it tends to put the taxonomist on edge.

In spite of the large number of species of "pinks" as they are frequently called, and an unusually colorful and rich history, pinks are not particularly common in American gardens. Therefore it might come as a bit of a shock to learn that during the past several hundred years, and mostly in England I gather, more than 27,000 *named* strains or cultivars have been produced. *27,000 names!*

This claim may be verified, by the stout-hearted, in *The International Dianthus Register*, Second Edition, 1983, The Royal Horticultural Society. [I freely admit that I have taken the word of Dr. A. C. Leslie, Registration Officer of The Royal Horticultural Society, who actually did the counting!] Beginning with dianthus 'Al' and ending with dianthus 'Zurich,' this list attempts to record names used to distinguish almost all known forms of dianthus. And this list is admittedly "not complete [but] it is believed that the great majority of plants raised and named in the United Kingdom . . . have now been accounted for." I think, quite possibly, that the rest of the world might best be left uncounted for now. There is quite enough to remember as it is.

My view of names began to flounder, actually, neither with tulips nor with pinks but with daylilies. I have enjoyed daylilies for many years, but lately when perusing garden catalogs it has seemed so difficult to choose any one particular plant to order. All the descriptions seem to be the same in fact, yet no two catalogs even remotely offer the same cultivars for sale. Where do they all come from one wonders?

I was somewhat shocked to discover the answer to this question late in 1983 when I read that some 24,000 named daylilies had been registered. A check made out of curiosity with Mr. W. E. Monroe, Registrar of the American Hemerocallis Society, confirmed this figure and raised it to 25,581 as of 31 December 1983.

This seems almost incredibly too productive to my poor way of thinking, especially when one considers that most of this development has taken place since the late 1800's. Mr. Monroe also stated that 6–700 cultivars are introduced each year.

I find this just a bit extravagant. I mean the normal sort of gardening person would be doing well to plant a half-dozen daylilies in his garden—perhaps even his lifetime. I am quite fond of them, as I've said, but I grow scarcely more than a dozen kinds (and these mostly from seed). I'd like to know who has the other 25,569?

One could go on and on, of course, counting the names of rhododendrons and azalea cultivars (15,000), irises (almost 50,000), or roses (15,000). But where would that get us I wonder—just slightly more confused? Which is just the point, I think, because things are quite confused enough as they are.

If we concern ourselves solely with scientific names, as some are wont to do, then we have the simple problem of misidentification either of material we buy or receive from others as well as the material we give out. Often mistakes in names are due to carelessness (I know this from personal experience), but I suspect in some groups of plants with large numbers of species the problem is often innocent ignorance. For whom amongst us are botanical experts enough to recognize a mistake in scientific nomenclature let alone to rectify it? Misinformation, it might seem, would be easily perpetuated.

Cultivar names are far worse in my opinion because there are by all counts too many of them. It is inconceivable to me that any hybridizer could recognize more than a few hundred of his own varieties, never mind the other hundreds or thousands in existence. For example, of the 25,000 (or so) daylily hybrids developed in the past century, probably about 5000 are still in trade. I would like to grow all 5000 in my garden and have someone identify them by name. It would be a most interesting, but unfair, test.

In reality I am not so callous about hybridizers as all of this might appear. They are truly dedicated individuals who are enjoying themselves. It is the garden writers, rather, who irk me. Especially the newspaper and magazine columnists who tell us what we "must have" in order to be proper gardeners. Who has not read this standard gardening prose: "I consider among my most favorite of *all* daylilies the delightfully smouldering, luscious peach-pink dwarf form of 'Unyielding Brutal Passion,' undoubtedly the best form available today. You really must have this in your garden." Contrived deadline nonsense is all it is. To know which is the best of 5000 names one would have to know all of the cultivars. And as anyone knows who has ever tried to find even a single cultivar mentioned in a column, it can't be done. Rather it would be more honest to say: "Of the three daylilies personally known to me, 'Left-handed Wrench' is perhaps the most interesting." The plant will still be impossible to find, mind you, and will in no way differ from 'Celestial Ooze,' 'Charming Bimbo,' or 'Nutcracker's Revenge,' but at least the prose will be honest.

Yes, entirely too much fuss is made about names. Names are nice, of course, but plants are nicer, so it is the plant with which we should be most concerned. We should perhaps adopt the policy that names are only a rippling reflection of reality and not reality itself. A guideline not a gilded name-card. For what we take as fact is not always what it seems, even when we "call it by some better name."

19
Gardeners: An Appreciation

If ever I were given a chance to live in the Garden of Eden—a most unlikely event, indeed—I would not accept. First because I love apples too much, and second because with my luck I'd be the only one there.

It does a gardener scarcely any good at all to have raised, let us say, the finest snapdragon known to humankind, if said gardener is the only one around to admire it. Most gardeners are far too busy gardening to admire their own plants, and psychologically it is probably not proper. It is far better, actually, to appear to ignore one's own paltry efforts at gardening while applauding those of others. And if the game is played correctly, when our gardening friends come to visit they will behave reciprocally. It is quite poor form not to.

It has often been asked, though in a slightly different form, "if a garden grew in the forest would anyone see it?" Of course I can not completely explain the answer to this question as it is far too complex for a non-technical book such as this. But I can state in simple, non-technical terms that the answer is "no." Unless, of course, you are there in which case the answer is usually "yes." These apparently complex philosophical matters often have a very simple answer (or even two)— it is only when one tries to explain them that the difficulties arise.

To rephrase the entire argument in terms that even I might understand, there is not much sense in having a garden unless some-one else is there to enjoy it. We, ourselves, are usually too busy to notice

the few good parts, and whatever else might be said about self-motivation, the psychological effects of positive comments to (and from) other gardeners cannot be overstated. We need gardening friends and they need us. And so I feel no guilt whatsoever in introducing you to several of the gardeners who have made a difference in my gardening. These are not the gardening sorts whom the writers are always citing as the great gardeners of their time . . . not the Jekylls or Robinsons . . . but rather the gardeners who have helped us the most. Namely our peers.

The first gardener who comes to mind does so because yesterday opened the annual manuring of the garden . . . or more correctly the official opening of the pile season. For firstly the manure must be collected and then dumped before it can be spread—an operation that requires several weekends of loading and unloading. Then comes several months (to years) of moving from drive-way to garden, cartload by cartload. (This was explained in great detail in Chapter 8 in case you missed it.)

It seems like a herculean task just to do my few sniveling truckloads each year, yet the fellow who owns the truck does dozens and dozens of such moves for his gardening friends. And he doesn't charge a cent, not even for gas. Why, he doesn't even own the horses. About all he gets from this hauling is pleasure—if you can call two fused discs and almost constant back problems as pleasure.

It used to be, when I first moved to my garden, that my friend Dug would show up in January and personally dump a year's supply of horse droppings in my driveway. To some this would be anathema . . . but not to a gardener. This happened for a year or two, and I began to feel slightly guilty, somewhat as if I were taking advantage of a feeble-minded friend. I especially began to feel guilty when he went to the hospital to have his back mended.

Finally I could stand the mental anguish no longer and I started helping Dug load and unload the truck when we gathered up my year's supply. This evolved into helping him with his personal requirements (which were more than prodigious), and eventually into delivering down the street, across town, and over to the next county. While it is generally nice to have friends, I sometimes wonder if it is absolutely necessary. (For further mention of this philosophical conundrum see "reciprocal work equation," Chapter 5.)

To put the exploits of this grand gardening figure even more into perspective I should point out a few of the real-life conditions under which these manure-hauling endeavors take place. First off they occur in the family Blazer (his family, I might add) not some open-to-the-air, pick-up truck. The rear seat is removed, the back window is rolled down and the inside is filled to overflowing. Dung balls and straw roll or cascade over and between the front seats like some murky avalanche. This dung, I might add, is on the edge of fermentation with great clouds of steam rising from the pile outside while inside the truck a perfect ammonia sauna is created. After reaching maximum capacity (i.e., so the driver can see out the front window with only a modicum of discomfort), Dug climbs in and steams himself for the 5 or 10 minutes (sometimes half-hour) ride to the delivery point.

After only a few minutes of steeping in the truck, anyone would smell like a knight who slept with his horses—a point which is amply made by gazing in the awe-struck eyes of anyone who is fortunate enough to receive the dung hauler. After 4 or 5 hours of hauling (and steeping), the physical greetings are about as intricate as if one were a leper giving out handfuls of hundred dollar bills. The reception, shall we say, is enthusiastically restrained.

Expert dung-handlers like Dug apparently get used to this cultural queasiness, but I, as a novice, still feel socially ostracized upon making a delivery. I hunker towards the back of the load and keep myself well downwind of the recipient and new keeper of the piles. When I finish for the day, I rush home, bowl over the cats (who, anxiously awaiting dinner, decide that eating is not really as necessary as breathing and depart at all due haste), strip off all my clothes, throw them down the basement steps, and fall into the shower gasping for fresh air.

Dug, on the other hand, being the consummate expert, goes home, has a glass of wine or two, and generally lounges around the house trying to figure out where his wife and daughters might have gone. Odd, isn't it, how they are never home on one of Dug's dung days?

As you might suspect of anyone who covers their property under truckloads of manure, Dug's garden is exceptional in its exuberance. Great beds of annuals are one of its trademarks, but there is also an honest-to-goodness rock garden, a large pond (and several small "water holes"), a hardy cactus garden, a moveable, tender cactus garden, grape and clematis trellises, a fruit orchard, a lath house, and a greenhouse—all on a suburban lot of less than one-quarter acre.

For years Dug and his wife Judy also planted a positively huge vegetable garden on soil at the top of the hill behind their house. The soil did not legally belong to them but they treated the earth as if it did, faithfully incorporating an annual dressing of horse manure and creating enough produce to open a farmers' market. (They now have permanent custody of the land having saved it from the developer's bulldozer.)

Gardeners, although terribly self-reliant and independent, do have a gregarious streak in them. Even if it is only mildly self-indulgent we like people to come and admire our current triumphs of the gardening art. And so it is with Dug and me. At least once a month (at least before he became a government administrator) we each pay the other an inspection visit. With some gardeners such a visit might be on a one-upmanship basis, but not with us. We are proud to have anything at all to brag about, even if it is just a single marigold. Perhaps because the two of us are different sorts of gardeners there is no sense of competition between us.

Dug exemplifies one of the most likable qualities of a gardener, namely generosity. Whether it be in quantities of time or excess of

plants, in reciprocal watering agreements or mutual admiration societies, gardeners give of themselves and generally get on well with each
other. Too bad we couldn't replace all the world's politicians with
gardeners. Then we'd really be getting some place.

* * * *

There are many twists and turns on life's roads, and it would
seem at times as if we have little control over our own sense of direction. For example, a few decades ago (nearly three to be painfully truthful) as I was walking to the playground in the new neighborhood to
which we had just moved, I saw a house astride the crest of a hill. It was
framed all around by trees, rhododendrons, and azaleas except for a
huge rock garden that cascaded from the house nearly three-fourths of
the way to the street where I stood. The rockery seemed enormous at
the time and somewhat mysterious as well, for it could only be glimpsed
in bits and pieces through the hill's greenery. I noted mentally that I
would like to investigate this place of intrigue further, then ran off mind-
lessly to play.

Not long after this pass-by, as if by some prearranged schedule,
its owners dropped by my parents' house. They had learned of my interest in natural history through an article in the local paper and thought I
might be talked into working in their garden. I think perhaps things
were meant to be this way.

I worked in this garden for a number of years with an almost
invariable preciseness which included 2 hours of watering on Mondays,
Wednesdays, and Fridays and miscellaneous chores on Saturdays. Here
I learned pruning and weeding, stump removal and weeding, potting-
up and weeding, pot-scrubbing and weeding, planting and weeding,
and weeding and weeding. Actually I learned the basics of gardening in
this garden, but that was scarcely anything at all compared to the
inspiration and enthusiasm that its founders instilled in me. If I am a
gardener (a dubious notion at best) it is because I spent a great many
years in the presence of real honest-to-earth gardeners.

The garden of which I write began in the 1930's on the side of a
typically golden California hill north of San Francisco. From old photos
it is clear that it was an exposed garden—hot and dry except for a
towering clump of bay towards the back of the property. Many of the
surrounding and surviving hills are exactly the same today as then. Yet

through the efforts of two gardeners, today a rhododendron and azalea preserve lies nestled amongst numerous towering trees.

Its creators are Coulter and Virginia Stewart, names well known amongst San Francisco plant connoisseurs. [Although Coulter passed away several years ago his presence in the garden is still very much felt.] Of the two, Coulter was the thorough and precise gardener and Virginia the more retentive and omnivorous one. Between them they shared a love and encyclopedic knowledge of plants unsurpassed by any gardeners known to me. They also set rather remarkable examples of plantsmanship which one may envy but few could emulate.

Coulter, for example, always the stickler for detail and a rabid rhododendron fancier, decided that he should follow the new system of nomenclature for rhododendron species proposed in 1980. At the age of 72 this meant unlearning his previous 50 years of acquired knowledge and replacing it with the new. Not an easy task for anyone, especially a person not particularly well versed in taxonomic botany. Yet he did it and was able to keep the younger "pups" on the right path when they unknowingly strayed off into the nomenclatural abyss.

Coulter did not espouse newness for newness' sake, quite the contrary. Something had to prove its merit before he might adopt its use. With plant labels, for instance, he would run controlled tests to see which labels with which writing implements and which fixatives would last longest in the garden. [I still have the labels he sent years ago to test under our harsh eastern conditions.]

He would have none of the elegant (and time-saving) underground automatic sprinkler systems for the simple fact that they did not respect the wishes of individual plants. So watering was done by hand, or with small spot sprinklers, or with large impulse sprinklers depending upon the time honored test of time.

And of gadget tools he had no use whatsoever. A simple, well built tool with *you* as the only moving part was his ideal. All of the fence-mending, lath house and greenhouse building, house repair, and general all-around puttering was done by hand with hand tools . . . some of which he inherited from his father.

Everything was done right the first time even if it took years. When I first started working for the Stewarts, they had a lath house perched on the side of the hill. This house was about a quarter-century old and was beginning to bend a little (both this-a-way and that). Its time had obviously come and a few little repairs would not have forestalled the inevitable. However it continued to serve its purpose for the next several years while it was slowly enclosed within the walls of a brand new redwood and fiberglass greenhouse. The greenhouse grew slowly so as not to disturb the benchfuls of plants inside. Excavations were made in the prone position under benches or in the billy-goat position on the side of the hill. Hand-carried block was set onto hand-poured foundations, made from hand-mixed concrete, and mortared with hand-mixed mortar (a bucketful at a time). Eventually, when the time came and the greenhouse was completed, the lath house was removed so quickly from inside that the plants scarcely knew that anything had happened.

When I worked with Coulter we were the heavy laborers of the garden. Digging, hauling, moving . . . that sort of job. Conversation was at a minimum and usually centered around correcting some remark or other that I had just made . . . Coulter was precise and usually correct.

When I worked with Virginia we did the finesse jobs of the garden—weeding, repotting, planting out. With Virginia conversation was at a maximum and almost invariably revolved about plants. If there is anyone who knows more about plants I have not met them. Nor about old-time Bay Area nurserymen. Virginia knows them all and I do believe she can still recall every trip to every nursery that she ever took, the name of every plant she ever bought, and the price (not to mention the color of the flowerpot). (It is, quite frankly, an embarrassment for me to be with Virginia on occasion. She may be telling me in great detail, for instance, about a nursery that we visited in September of 1963 and the plants we both bought and I will be furiously counting on my fingers trying to calculate if I was even alive that year).

In the Stewart garden there has always been some specialty or other of prominent interest, whether it ranged from the generalities of South African bulbs or the specifics of pleione culture, from pelargonium cultivars to football-sized chrysanthemums, or from azaleas to primroses. These specialties were invariably the province of Virginia who acquired new cultivars with a studied calmness and who calmly studied each plant until its name, color, shape, and idio-syncrasies were filed away never to be forgotten. These were not passing fancies but well-cultivated friends who lived on and on for years before gradually and grudgingly giving way to yet newer friends. (They never seemed particularly friendly to me, however, because there were always hundreds of plants in pots, requiring endless watering and endless pot-washing. Pots lined the driveway and upper pathways and always, I thought, got in the way of watering. I had to take great care not to wrap the hose around a plant and pull it crashing over onto its head. Hose dragging is still an art I have yet to conquer.)

Among Virginia's specialties falls the category of rock garden plants . . . a generality if ever there was one. Almost every family of plant could produce an example of the "rock-garden-variety," so it is not really so much a specialty as an approach. Fine points notwithstanding, Virginia has always been a strong proponent of rock gardens and their plants. A long-time member of both the U.S. and English rock garden societies (and once honorary vice-president of the former), it was Virginia's responsibility to fill up the lath house (and later the greenhouse) that Coulter so dutifully provided.

Once, before my time, Virginia had sown seeds of *Cyclamen hederifolium* from which she not only grew a quantity of garden plants but about which she also wrote a 1950 article for the *Bulletin* of the American Rock Garden Society (quoted later in Elizabeth Lawrence's book entitled *The Little Bulbs,* Criterion Books, 1957). A few cyclamen planted out nearly 40 years ago have now become a dell of marbled foliage and flowers covering 30 to 40 square feet. By seeding and reseeding (naturally) they have taken hold of a once dry patch of California hillside beneath a towering pine . . . reminiscent, perhaps, of a spot on one of the cyclamen's Mediterranean islands. This recreation of a wild colony represents one of the rare sorts of gardening triumphs possible only to those who spend a lifetime in one garden. Such gardens are certainly not for the faint of heart, nor the impatient.

While 40 years is probably a bit longer wait than most gardeners will accept, perhaps waiting 15 years for a rhododendron seedling to bloom is more amenable. Then again, I doubt it . . . most of us think three weeks from seed to flower is quite long enough. Coulter and Virginia have been rhododendron enthusiasts for more years than I've known myself. The average run-of-the-mill year of late has seen some 300 or so rhododendrons and azaleas liberally drifted throughout the garden. A striking fact when one considers that a more unlikely candidate for a hot, dry climate scarcely can be imagined. (We gardeners have never claimed great intelligence, just great determination.) The fiercest rays of the direct sun have been eliminated by now stately conifers (once minuscule saplings) which replace direct heat above ground with rapid water depletion beneath. Several years back, during a great drought and water-rationing summer in the 70's, thousands of dollars worth of water had to be trucked in from the next county to keep the rhododendrons from dying. Many a lesser gardener might have used the money for a vacation . . . or even to move.

Yet in spite of great odds and unlikely and harsh conditions, the Stewart rhododendrons have won numerous trophies, plates, cups, ribbons, and assorted bric-a-brac . . . enough, in fact, to fill up the greenhouse if it weren't for the good fortune that all the metalwares have been rotating awards. Virginia has evolved into a judge, herself, of the various chapter shows that are held in the San Francisco Bay region. She carries with her a keen eye for detail and a storehouse of knowledge filled, like here greenhouse, to overflowing.

I do not suppose Virginia will mind if I make a final comment about rhododendrons . . . at least one or two cultivars in particular. For some years now (since 1972) the rhododendron 'Virginia Stewart' has been winning best-in-show awards for its great white flower trusses. This cultivar was first grown and recognized by Coulter and Virginia from hybrid seedlings created by a long-time friend of theirs. After con-

siderable time and effort Coulter formally registered the cultivar and it is now being introduced to the trade. Conversely, Virginia will be registering a hybrid rhododendron herself sometime soon—one that Coulter grew. I will leave it to your imagination as to what it might be named. I imagine it will not be long before I have both 'Virginia' and 'Coulter Stewart' growing in my garden (or at least my greenhouse).

Coulter and Virginia personify the gardening spirit: patient beyond years, undemanding yet ever-hopeful, stubbornly optimistic. Qualities we might all strive towards, perhaps too highly set for some, but worth the attempt. We would do well from time to time to cultivate our fellow gardeners as we do our garden for they are a source of inspiration we should never be without.

20
Gardens: An Affirmation

I think it says a lot about gardeners that we gain as much (usually more) emotional satisfaction by visiting the gardens of others as we do from our own paltry attempts at tilling the earth. Perhaps it is because as a whole we seem to be a self-deprecating lot; we invariably reduce our own garden to a state of "you-should-have-seen-it-last-month." But whereas we are never quite satisfied with our own work, we always seem to find the good parts of everyone else's. And we do it without envy. (Greed, however, is another matter indeed, and I will not willfully be enticed into that discussion except to point out that there must be a notable ethical difference between grievous envy and a simple case of "finger blight." I do not know, myself, exactly what this difference is, but intuitively any gardener can verify its existence.)

In truth I enjoy visiting the gardens of others because it is so instructive. One can always pick-up a good idea, or a new plant, or even an unthought-of combination of well-known plants. (One can even learn how not to do things, but again, that is another story.) Even if I were to learn nothing, I often take great pleasure in knowing that I am not home slaving away in my own garden.

In the United States, garden-visiting is neither an art nor a great social experience by any means, and is, in fact, essentially non-existent. Certainly visits are paid to larger botanical gardens and arborata. But I do not consider these so much gardens as extravaganzas. No, what I mean are visits to our neighbors' or friends' gardens or even those of other townsfolk.

We do not see, for example, neatly hand-crafted signs along our streets proclaiming "Garden Open Today" with a little cup set on a stool and a gate-fee for the grand sum of 25p marked on a card. No, these certainly would not be seen in the United States, but such gardens are typically found in England. These are the gardens of The National Gardens Scheme, gardens which almost universally belong to private citizens who wish (one presumes) to show off their garden (just a bit, perhaps) and to turn any proceeds (at 10 or 25 or even 80p a whack) over to this Trust originally founded as a benevolent fund for District Nurses.

As I have briefly alluded to in the previous chapter, I do occasionally visit my fellow gardeners, the nearest of whom is two miles away, and I do so with great personal pleasure. I must admit, however, that in all fairness such visits could never be matched by a single pilgrimage I once made to the acknowledged mecca of all gardeners and to my own personal rendezvous with the unknown. The journey was made once and shall never be made again; it need not be, nor indeed, cannot be.

Sudbrook Cottage

And there it stood, then. Three thousand miles by air, three miles by foot, and twenty-five years by way of anticipation. And there it stood: a white picket fence, a fading sign, and the words "Sudbrook Cottage." Just what I was doing here, standing in front of a fence which looked much like my own, was a mystery to me. My presence probably would have been equally as puzzling to the inhabitant of the cottage as well, if he had known I was there, that is. Oh, I had an invitation to be certain, but it was a somewhat unnerving one . . . that is to say one which was not quite as positive as it might have been. Earlier in the year, when I had requested permission to visit Sudbrook Cottage, the owner had replied as follows: "Hopefully I shall be dead next September but if you would like to ring up my number is. . . ."

The only clue by which I might possibly decipher such a message was to recall that of the 60-odd books (including 30 best sellers) the owner had written, smoldering satire was a trademark. Never lacking in opinion, nor style, nor especially a keen choice of words (which even 50 years later overpower most of the sameness that passes as garden writing), the inhabitant of Sudbrook Cottage has been a

SUDBROOK COTTAGE

gardening inspiration for the past half-century. Which, I suppose, might take a little of the mystery out of why I was now standing at the front gate of Beverley Nichols of Ham, Surrey, England.

But still, my exact reasons for being here were uncomfortably vague. After all, I was supposed to "ring up" for an appointment and I hadn't done that. "But, suppose," I thought to myself, "that Mr. Nichols is really not well . . . it wouldn't do to 'ring up,' for I should only be disturbing him. Or, even worse, suppose that Mr. Nichols' hopes had been answered, in which case I shouldn't need to ring up at all." And standing now, in front of the gate, I feared the latter to be true. For Sudbrook Cottage appeared to have a certain air of finality to it. The windows gazed out at the common with a certain blankness; there was little comfort to be taken there. The tiny forecourt was plainly sad, to say the least. And the green, wooden door which had led countless visitors to the garden, appeared to be losing a battle against the waves of grass which flanked it. I stood there wondering why I had come all this way and then reluctantly walked away.

A few hundred feet beyond the cottage I sat down on a bench that was about as rickety as the 25 years of imagining which separated my youth from this moment. My thoughts turned to Mr. Nichols' recent autobiography entitled *The Unforgiving Moment* (1978), and I thought to myself, "it is the garden that is unforgiving, and his has given up on him. Just as mine will give up on me in the end; in fact while I am in England it will probably disappear forever. Why not stay home and tend to your own sadly neglected garden? Why tempt the safety of imagination with reality?" I could not answer these questions.

Instead, I slowly walked back to the cottage and stopped at the green door . . . the only means of entry into the garden from the common. The door had a knob in the middle and was surrounded by a 7 ft. brick wall beyond which only the mind could see. Perhaps I had come here merely to harvest some mysterious seed sown when I was 13, the year I first read *Down the Garden Path*. Perhaps I had nurtured the ethereal garden too long, and in too idyllic a place, to accept what I actually saw. The outer landscape was too bleak, both physically and mentally; the only possible hope was the green door that stood before me and what might lay beyond. "What sort of garden," I thought, "could possibly be confined behind that immense wall and behind that locked door? Why do the English surround themselves with walls of such greatness? So no one can see the weeds? Perhaps the reason that the British are such good gardeners," I thought, "is because no one ever sees anyone else's garden. Could this superiority all be hearsay?"

It was at this moment of incipient derangement that reason finally persuaded me to do the sensible thing. I would simply have to make an appointment to see what lay beyond the door. After 25 years of imaginary gardening I had developed an indefinable need to see what must be seen.

And so, later that week, a call was made. "Yes, please do come," was Mr. Nichols' reply. "Tea at four, shall we say. Saturday a week." And Saturday a week I was there, again standing at the picket fence with the little white sign. A ring of the bell, an eon of apprehension, muffled scufflings, assorted bangings, the door opening slowly, Mr. Nichols standing in the doorway, and me struck simultaneously numb and dumb. "Please excuse my apparel," he said lightly of his walker, and I was invited within. We ambled down a darkened hall, both of us rather wobbly, due in varying degrees to age and infirmity on his part, and an attack of nervous limbs on mine.

Quickly, however, apprehension was abandoned as I caught my first glimpse of the garden. Through the drawing room door I could see a most impeccably manicured lawn, surrounded by an enticing tartan of coniferous greens. As we moved closer to the doorway I spied the green door of my first exploratory visit; could the garden door I now viewed, this door surrounded by paradise, could this be the same door I had seen on the outside? It was, and I could not believe the contrast.

We stepped shakily into the garden, from the darkness into light, the two of us. Into an unusually warm, sun-filled afternoon. Mr. Nichols took my arm for support and quite cheerfully pointed to his triumphs while I revelled blissfully in them. This was the stuff that dreams were made of; dreams of youth which suffered nothing upon awakening. We walked slowly past a group of hardy cyclamen blooming in the shadow of the green door; past stately rhododendrons (no die-back or borrer here, in paradise); past tall-flowered sedum awash with bees and tortoise-shell butterflies on a sea of pink; past a crimson layer of dahlias held strongly above their purplish black cloaks (befitting the title 'Bishop of Llandaff'); beyond the kochia aching to break into flame at the first sign of fall; beyond the impatiens glowing in the benevolence of the British summer; and ending in the small bed of heathers with their purplish extremities flung wantonly into the air. It was a simple selection of flowers, planted as a broad, sweeping curve backed by an array of entwined conifers. The foreground was an elegant lawn, tightly rolled and closely clipped putting any putting green to shame.

Standing here, it seems appropriate (in retrospect) to pause momentarily and consider Sudbrook Cottage and the garden which Beverley Nichols has created. The story of this particular garden was told in his two books entitled *Garden Open Today* (1963) and *Garden Open Tomorrow* (1968), and I need not compete with those tomes of garden prose. However Mr. Nichols stressed three principles of garden design in the first book about Sudbrook Cottage, and it would be useful to review them here. Simply stated they are: 1) there must be a body of water in the garden; 2) a garden is doubled in size by being cut in half; and 3) the beauty of a square garden depends upon curves, and the beauty of an irregular garden begins with squares. The two of us had just walked along one of the sweeping curves which took the edge off the acre-square, walled garden, and we now had reached the point where the garden was halved. This was accomplished by the intrusion of a bold curve of conifers into the lawn. Piercing this green wall were several steps which were flanked on either side by urns. A path could be seen above the steps and this appeared to lead directly into a weeping cherry of no little size. Nothing else could be seen from this point, halfway from the house.

   We carefully mounted the steps and followed the path that now could be seen to veer off to the left of the cherry tree. The tree itself was rather a surprise as it was formed from three trees planted tightly together. The branch structure was so dense as to hide the trunks in a mound of leaves. Once beyond the cherries we came upon a small glen and a vista even more ethereal than the one I'd seen from the doorway. Here, hidden within walls of conifer and robinia, of cherry and holly, here was the main principle of the garden . . . water. We had come to the edge of a perfectly formal pool set amongst a perfectly informal garden. But what a garden it was . . . a theater in the round, framed against a nearly continuous backdrop of green tapestries. The pool sat close to us, a veritable stage dappled in late-day sunlight (and outlined, its owner quietly explained, in brick made by Daniel Defoe of Crusoe fame). Stage center stood our principle thespian in the character of a cheery cherub, and who among us would not be cheerful with this garden constantly before our eyes? Stage front sat a handsome leaded dolphin, perhaps awaiting some cue from its nearby co-star. To the left of the pool a planting of white and pale-green foliaged *Cornus* was complemented by a similar *Weigela;* a low-growing spirea added just a blush of pink to the scene. All were doubled in size by the trickery of mirrors which appeared to lie on the pool's surface. Clumps of Japanese iris rose gracefully through the water's film and these were reflected rather mysteriously by *Crocosmia* planted on the bank. In the audience, in addition to ourselves and the cluster of cherries, a few of the more remote seats were occupied by stately, variegated holly. Clusters of starch-white *Anaphalis* jostled the 'Bishop of Llandaff' for a better view of the stage. And overlooking the entire production was a most handsome specimen of a tall, yellow-foliaged false acacia *Robinia* × *Hillieri,* among the first specimens of its kind to be planted in England.

By this time we had sat down upon strategically placed benches . . . the best seats in the house, as it were, and we engaged in fits and snatches of gardener's talk. This went on for some few minutes, but it became apparent that Mr. Nichols was rapidly growing tired and that I had so many years of questions jumbled in my mind that I could scarcely get them unraveled, let alone ask them. Yet one question finally tumbled out, and it focused upon the previous garden about which Mr. Nichols had written. This 5-acre garden was immortalized in a series of three books beginning in 1951 with *Merry Hall,* followed in 1953 by *Laughter on the Stairs,* and in 1956 by *Sunlight on the Lawn.* More enjoyable garden reading simply does not exist, nor, alas, does the garden, for Mr. Nichols informed me that it had gone the way of the subdivision. He would not speak further of the matter, and, if he had tried, I would not have listened. Too much reality, at least in one sitting, is not good for the gardener.

It was time, now, to begin our trek back towards the green door. We had visited the primary focal points visible from the house, namely the long, curved border around the lawn and the sylvan glade at the top of the steps. For our return trip the focal point became the house itself, which was framed by an immense canopy of copper beech (one of the few remaining plantings which had come with the house in 1958). Beneath the tree, and subtending a crazy-pavement walk, several irregular clusters of green lay scattered in an informal woodland fashion: a patch of Solomon's Seal gazed diffidently across the way towards stately *Acanthus; Hamamelis* interrupted the lawn in spots; white and green *Lamium* flowed over the ground with an occasional and unsuspected foray upon the boundary of the well-kept lawn. And everywhere today's crop of beech nuts lay claim to the ground. It was but a short walk along the path, or so it seemed, and too soon we had reached the drawing room door. Mr. Nichols begged his leave to rest a moment and ready himself for yet another set of visitors.

I was left on my own, now, to retour the garden at leisure and to ponder the events of the afternoon. I wandered about for a while, stopping idly at the pool, taking photographs, gathering a few beech nuts, and wondering which I liked better, the garden or the book. Beverley Nichols' gardening books had cast a spell on me as a lad. His 40 years of garden prose speaks even today of times and places I would like to know; of cottages and manors, of city gardens and country, of people and plants. I had waited half a life to visit a dream and now I was reluctant to leave. But the sun was beginning to cast long shadows across the garden as it dipped over the wall, and I knew the time had come. The day had been warm and sunny, the air still (the sort of day when the air hangs about with nothing particular in mind); my favorite kind of a day, as a matter of fact. And this had been my favorite kind of a garden, I decided, a garden of affirmation; proof, as it were, that imagination does not always surpass reality. And standing now, before the green door which would return me to the outside, I decided that it didn't really matter which side of the door I faced. Even though I suspected one dream would end if I stepped through, I also realized that it would not matter.

Epilogue

In his book *Merry Hall,* Beverley Nichols commented:

> "I cannot forecast, with any accuracy, the probable nature of my own horticultural demise; at the moment in view of the fact that the water garden is claiming most of my attention, it will probably take the form of drowning. Indeed, by the time these words are published [1951], I may already have been discovered floating under a clump of James Brydon nymphaeas."

The year after I visited Mr. Nichols' garden and on the occasion of his 85th birthday, he suffered a fall and died a week later, 15 September 1983.

21
Gardening: An Institution

Gardeners are a grand breed—the facts are indisputable. If the world were ever left to them it would be back to working order within weeks . . . days even.

Why is it, then, that when someone confides to us that they, too, are gardeners we have the uneasy suspicion that they are not quite right in the head? We suspect that something has warped their psyche and nothing known to humankind will wrest it back into alignment.

I do not believe that gardeners go mad because of the garden itself, although there are those who might suggest so. A garden merely exists, after all. It offers no resistance except in the "tar-baby" mind of its owner. The garden will grow quite nicely without our help as plants have done for eons. It will look like hell, of course, but this is only a subjective opinion of the gardener; the only true resistance will be in the gardener's mind. The garden is the garden. How we react to it personally is not, after all, its fault but our own. We cannot condemn the garden when we have created it.

Some might say that the physical act of gardening leads to mental imbalance, but I find this hard to believe because gardening seems to be quite a health-inducing experience. Excessive limbering exercise, quantities of fresh, purified air, and minimal mental stimulation . . . all of these are greatly therapeutic to the body and the soul. Have you ever tried to count the number of knee-bends or ground push-ups you do in the course of a gardening exercise such as pulling weeds? It can't be done—the number is too high.

No. As far as I can ascertain, not a single living person has ever gone insane either because of the garden or the process of gardening. I imagine, rather, that it is insanity . . . pure and simple . . . that leads us down the garden's primrose paths. It could not seem to be otherwise.

As I tried to suggest at the beginning of this book, although the gardener's life rests precariously on the moment, it is shaped by memories of the past and expectations of the future. To be a gardener one must be continually out of synchronization with reality. I ask you, what better definition does one need of insanity?

A kitchen full of seedlings in February is as wonderful as any border in June. They are really the same thing, only slightly displaced by what we call time. In fall a paper bag of daffodil bulbs is perhaps even better than the bright yellow splash of spring. After all, the dried, dusty bulbs are a pill to purge the melancholy of an entire winter . . . their flowers but one of the fleeting taunts of spring. Are not plots and plans and piles of things a panacea for a precarious future that may or may not come to pass?

A terrace is built . . . three years of real-time work . . . all the while the back breaks as the owner's imaginary behind sits and savors the rewards of an imaginary vista. In 6 years I may have sat down almost 6 hours on the terrace, but in my mind I have spent years there. To the outsider . . . the disinterested onlooker . . . I have invested heavily of time and energy and money for the sake of 6 hours of relaxation. Little does the onlooker appreciate how often my mental butt has rested on that terrace. And what a great relief it was to do so.

I've plotted and planned and planted, created piles of every description, potted up the pathways, and shredded crickets all in the name of gardening. I've weeded the rupturewort endlessly, grown tomatoes for social acceptance, battled a few bulbs, and even had a thought or two on rare occasion. All for the sake of the garden. Yet it is still not exactly clear to me *why* I do these things—why anyone does them, as a matter of fact. Unless of course we're crazy.

Take this year, for instance. I've had several opportunities to travel to distant and exotic corners of the world (especially if I pay for the trips myself). But I can't. Well, at least not entirely . . . not really . . . not without great pangs of guilt that would haunt me everywhere I went and ruin my trip anyway. With a great deal of emotional soul searching and grinding of teeth I've decided I must forgo a trip to Italy and Greece because this year's seedlings will be sprouting just when I should be leaving. I'd lose a whole year in the garden if I don't plant those seeds. I guess it's not worth a trip to Greece. For similar reasons the trip to England is out as well (for the third year in a row). It would fall at a time when the seedlings need potting-up and I could certainly not find anyone willing to do that. Even if I potted them up before leaving it wouldn't work. I tried that one year. The year, in fact, that I actually did go to England. I returned to nearly 6 dozen auricula corpses. Twenty dollars worth of English hybrid seed that had air-dried to flawless perfection in the furnace room while I was visiting their birthplace. The absence of water on seedlings is impressive . . . especially 6 weeks worth. *That* taught me a valuable lesson about gardening and I rarely ever forget it: don't go anywhere when there are seeds to tend.

The trip out to the West Coast must be postponed, too, because the only month I can go is April and that is precisely the month I must stay home to ward off the first onslaught of weeds. If I don't get that very first crop, the garden is a disaster for the rest of the year. I'd never catch up.

177

May would be a good month to go somewhere except for one catch. May is when the garden normally looks its best. I can't be off somewhere, say in Uzbekestan, when the garden is at its best. That would almost (but not quite) defeat the purpose of having a garden.

I will definitely attempt to sneak a trip to India into the schedule later this summer . . . say between August's last gasp and the first burst of chrysanthemums. But it has taken all the willpower at my disposal to find even this crack in the gardening year. And by August I may well find that unsuspected problems will have caught up with me and force a postponement of the trip to some future, unspecified date. It would not surprise me too much.

Time is precious in the garden. Obsessively so. Scarcely ever is there a block of time that can't be put to better use in gardening, say, than traveling. Equally obsessive—perhaps more so—is money. Scarcely ever is there a sum of money that can't better be spent on gardening, say, than eating.

Gardeners spend inordinate amounts of money if they ever stop to think about it . . . which fortunately most do not. I once calculated that on average a home-grown tomato costs somewhere between $15 and $20 a piece, a stalk of broccoli nearly $50, a dozen roses close to $100, and a pound of zucchini $10. [For those who are curious, these figures are arrived at using the following system: First add up your monthly mortgage payments for one year. Add to that sum the cost of seeds and transplants, fertilizer, chemical warfare agents, soil amendments, mole traps, mulch, stakes, string, and tools (pro-rated for as many years as you've owned them). Then add the cost of 27 round-trips to the nearest garden center (there are convenient government charts that give average costs per mile), water for a year (at whatever rate you pay), and your labor (25¢ per hour and 60 hours per week is normal for a gardener). Finally, calculate the cost required to truck excess zucchini from the garden. Divide above total by numbers of tomatoes, broccoli, roses, etc. You may never garden again.]

Gardens cost money. Lots of money. A fence, a bench, a bird-bath, a stake, a path, a package of seeds, a rock . . . everything costs dearly. But we eventually must have it in some form or other, or our garden will be incomplete.

Right now, as I sit in a newly built room, recently added to the house, my mind wanders off to the newly built greenhouse just outside. It has newly built benches made from costly new materials. Benches built to last my lifetime—sturdy, rigid. Able to withstand the pressures of tons of soil and gravel, of pots and plants and water.

Inside I write at a dining room table that totters on the edge of disaster. The slightest jostle will send piles of newspapers, books, garden catalogs, bills, and letters to the floor. (Bruno, as always, is desperately searching for some clear space to land . . . a certain disaster should it come to pass, as it invariably will.)

Outside there are new fans and thermostats, new flower pots, a new propagating bench with heating cables. New benches with expensive wire shelving—outside. I've been agonizing for weeks between buying an oak bench to put in the garden or a new oak desk to replace the dining room table as a place to write. The choice should seem simple, but for some reason it isn't.

Inside my new room has only the dining table. Next to the new room is an old room with a tattered and torn sofa that desperately cries out for replacement. The downstairs needs refurbishing and the upstairs needs demolition.

But outside I *do* have a working propagation bench and it propagates even as I write. I ask you which is more important, the sofa or the cutting? The desk or the bench? There would seem to be only one answer.

Again, which is more important—the body or the soul? My friend Dug gardens wearing a back brace (if he is good) when he shouldn't garden at all. He's already had one back operation and probably deserves another. Yet he would rather garden than not, and he is probably not alone. How many gardeners are there with bad backs, bad knees, bad elbows, bad minds? Lots. But you can't keep them from the garden. Even a herd of malpractice-suited doctors can't stay these gardeners from their appointed rounds.

The garden is a dangerous place even when we might think we know what we're doing. I have an acquaintance who nearly lopped off a finger whilst pruning his hedge. I've come close as well, painfully close. Through stupidity of course, or perhaps preoccupation (I was weeding at the time). But then stupidity is merely stupidity, after all, and not really a great substitute for missing fingers.

I know of no one who has fatally destroyed themselves in the garden (I suppose it happens now and again). But minor discomforts abound: sore and pulled muscles, sprains of the fingers, sunburn, poison oak and poison ivy, bee stings, cuts, scrapes, bruises, and rose bushes. We've suffered them all. I've fallen seat-first into a bed of beaver-tail cactus (not much fun, that); backwards onto the cutting edge of a flower pot; and headfirst into a hedgerow of multiflora rose. There is scarcely any part of me (and I do mean *any part*) that hasn't been pierced at some time or other by some plant, or knife, or bee or wasp or other.

One certainly does not set out voluntarily to destroy oneself . . . it just happens. Bruises appear as if by magic, usually days after we've been anywhere near a blunt object. Fingers start to fester where the tip of a rose thorn has broken off and the body begins to disengage it. Back muscles spasm midweek, miles from the garden, while we sit at a staff meeting trying to look normal but appearing rather more like some contortionist practicing for his next performance. (Several gardeners with whom I work have stood through past such meetings seeking hard-to-find relief.)

Somewhere in the standard gardener's contract . . . that is our papers of indenture . . . all of this pain and suffering stuff must be spelled out in great detail. I would guess that it is in very fine print, however, because I don't recall having seen it before. Perhaps it is stuck somewhere between the clause that reads ". . . neither shall ye be permitted the vexatiousness and idlity of time-off, nor shall ye cast bread upon vast waters of international kinds, nor frolic in exotic places with but little clothing on" and the one that states ". . . if riches be forthcoming verily toss them unto the soil of the earth, foul not thy living spaces with comforts, but forsake all material goods so that rutabagas and turnips may spring forth."

But wait, I *have* found it after all—that part about pain. It's in very tiny print. So tiny, in fact, as to need a microscope. But it is there nonetheless: "Make thy body a fortress of pain so that no man, nor woman even, shall have cause to say you do not suffer greatly in the name of the garden. *In pain shall the truth be known.*" Actually I don't care for the truth all that much. Not so you'd notice anyway. I mean pain is pain and truth is truth. I don't see much relationship between the two.

If the truth about gardener's insanity were really to become known I think it would not be pain that caused it to be so. Not pain, not time, not even money. None of these things by themselves, but a synergism of all three catalyzed by one final ingredient—work. *Work* is the diagnostician's key to the self . . . to the mind of the gardener. Therein lies a sign that points the way to insanity. Work. Pain may show us truth, but work shows us the true self.

Truth and pain, for example do not fertilize the lawn—I do. (Well, to be truthful I don't, but that's beside the point. I would fertilize the lawn if I did that sort of thing, but I am philosophically opposed to it. So I don't. But as this is an allegorical exploration into the psyche of a gardener's mind . . . or what's left of it . . . I bring up fertilizing the lawn as a point of rhetoric. I am interested here only in the philosophical interactions of truth and work. The fact that I am truthfully opposed to some sorts of work is immaterial.)

But let us return to the lawn. To fertilize the lawn is to make the lawn grow. No one in their right mind would want to make the lawn grow because that means you just have to cut it more often. I am morally opposed to such make-work projects on religious grounds . . . there is enough work to do without them.

I do all the work around here. The planning and planting (and replanting when the plans don't work), the seed sprouting and potting-up, the weeding, pruning, stump removal, watering, grass cutting, path-finding, stone masonry, wall construction, fence building, earth moving, graveling, plumbing, compost sifting, pond cleaning, and other odd-

jobs as necessary. And they *are* necessary.

These jobs are eternal, never-ending. They must all be done; to neglect any part results in collapse of the whole. To accomplish the whole results in a collapse of the gardener. But it must be so. There is certainly no need to invent work—it is generating spontaneously. Even as we weed one bed another cries for water, and while we water that one, weeds begin to regrow in the first. As we are sleeping in our own bed the garden is plotting against us. Planning out the next day's work for "the keeper." The garden never rests . . . never gives up.

It gives us no time-off (even for good behavior). It requires us to make sacrifices to it by digging holes and throwing money in them. It causes us to suffer miserably from self-inflicted pain. And it demands never-ending, almost thankless work for which one receives neither money nor rarely compliments. A person would have to be nearly crazy to work under these conditions.

And that just about sums up gardening.